本课题受到以下项目资助

◎中国科学院国际合作局项目

“支持 GRC 开放获取行动计划的世界开放获取行动评价与监测平台”（Y140321001）

◎中国科学院科学传播局、发展规划局项目

“中国科学院文献情报和期刊出版领域引进优秀人才计划”择优支持项目（Y14341001）

◎国家自然科学基金委项目

“开放获取重大趋势与科学基金相关政策研究”（ZK16041001）

开放获取知识库联盟（COAR）简介

Margaret Kathleen Shearer　主审

顾立平　编

科学技术文献出版社
SCIENTIFIC AND TECHNICAL DOCUMENTATION PRESS

·北京·

图书在版编目(CIP)数据

开放获取知识库联盟（COAR）简介 / 顾立平编. —北京：科学技术文献出版社，2016. 9（2017. 10 重印）

ISBN 978-7-5189-1879-9

Ⅰ. ①开… Ⅱ. ①顾… Ⅲ. ①开放存取—知识库—介绍—世界 Ⅳ. ① G253.1

中国版本图书馆 CIP 数据核字（2016）第 215996 号

开放获取知识库联盟（COAR）简介

策划编辑：崔灵菲　责任编辑：王瑞瑞　责任校对：张吲哚　责任出版：张志平

出 版 者　科学技术文献出版社
地　　址　北京市复兴路15号　邮编 100038
编 务 部　（010）58882938，58882087（传真）
发 行 部　（010）58882868，58882874（传真）
邮 购 部　（010）58882873
官方网址　www.stdp.com.cn
发 行 者　科学技术文献出版社发行　全国各地新华书店经销
印 刷 者　虎彩印艺股份有限公司
版　　次　2016 年 9 月第 1 版　2017 年 10 月第 3 次印刷
开　　本　850 × 1168　1/32
字　　数　70千
印　　张　4.125
书　　号　ISBN 978-7-5189-1879-9
定　　价　48.00元

前 言

开放获取知识库联盟（Confederation of Open Access Repositories, COAR）是一个迅速成长的国际联盟，它成立于2009年10月并且联合了全球100多家机构，旨在构建一个连接全球开放获取知识库的知识基础设施，以扩大科学研究成果的可见度，促进科学研究成果的广泛应用。本书汇集最近几年来COAR发布的几份重要文件，在某种程度上，说明了全球机构知识库的发展态势和目标。

本书从国际知识库的发展现状入手，介绍和分析了开放知识数据库的发展和重要作用，以及面临的挑战和机遇。重点介绍COAR的概念、加入COAR能够获取的权益及如何成为COAR会员。列举近年来COAR为强化构建全球开放获取知识空间的目标所做出的实践和努力，包括提出路线、草案、准则、会议、合作等，归纳COAR近些年所取得的成果，结合具体战略目标分析介绍COAR未来几年的发展方向和工作计划。本书中结合实际解答了关于COAR的常见问题，包括COAR的活动及成为会员的相关问题等。全书中英文结合，整体上帮助读者较为全面地认识 COAR 组织、功能、已有成果、发展方向等。

本书摘取自 COAR 及 Margaret Kathleen Shearer 的手稿；顾立平统筹，负责遴选、组织编译和校对；最终稿件由 Margaret Kathleen Shearer 主审。参与各章节贡献的人员如下：第 1 章由张嘉欣和段美珍编译，段美珍和王振蒙完成校对；第 2 章，2.1 节由张嘉欣编译和王振蒙校对，2.2 节由王振蒙编译和张嘉欣校对，2.3 节由李丽梅编译和郭进京校对，2.4 节由郭进京编译和张梦霞校对，2.5 节由宋忠惠编译和段美珍校对，2.6 节由段美珍编译和赵越校对，2.7 节由彭乃珠编译和王振蒙校对；第 3 章，3.1 节由张嘉欣编译和郭进京校对，3.2 节由赵越编译和张晓丹校对，3.3 节由李丽梅校对和赵越编译；第 4 章由张晓丹编译和李丽梅校对；第 5 章由杨小薇完成编译；本书全部内容由段美珍统稿，交付顾立平再次校对，并且委由杨良斌通读整理，史盈盈和丁利芳参与编辑。

本书知识内容的贡献者是 Margaret Kathleen Shearer 女士。对中文编译内容付出主要贡献的是杨小薇老师、杨良斌老师等上述参与人员，本书若有任何缺失、不足之处，应属编者顾立平之责任。本书的形成得益于以上参与者的合作，本书实施开放获取。

Content

1 Current State of Repositories 1

1.1 Executive Summary 1

1.2 Introduction 3

1.3 Repository Demographics 5

1.4 Regional Repository Networks 8

1.5 Challenges and Opportunities 21

1.6 Conclusions 30

2 Practice and Effort of COAR 32

2.1 COAR Published Interoperability Roadmap 32

2.2 COAR Launches Draft "Resource Type" Vocabulary for Open Access Repositories 37

2.3 COAR Joined Europe's OpenAIRE 2020 to Strengthen International Collaboration 39

2.4 COAR @ IFLA World Library and Information Congress 2015 41

2.5 La Referencia Adopted OpenAIRE Guidelines 43

2.6 COAR Guidelines for Assessing Publisher Repository Services 45

2.7 Reinforce the Aim to Develop a Global, Open Access Knowledge Commons 47

3 Cooperation and Achievement of COAR 49

3.1 Major Repository Networks Agree to Collaborate 49

3.2 The Sustainable Development Goals E-forum Discussion... 51

3.3 Major Repository Networks Agree to Adopt Common Guidelines 53

4 Development Strategy and Plan 58

4.1 COAR Strategy 2016-2018 58

4.2 COAR Work Plan 2016-2017 59

目 录

1 国际知识库现状 66

1.1 报告摘要 66

1.2 前言 67

1.3 知识库统计特征 69

1.4 区域知识库网络 72

1.5 挑战和机遇 81

1.6 报告结论 87

2 COAR 的实践与努力 89

2.1 COAR 发布知识库互操作路线图 89

2.2 COAR 启动制定控制词表草案 93

2.3 COAR 参与欧洲 OpenAIRE 2020 以强化国际合作 94

2.4 COAR 执行董事出席 2015 年国际图联大会 96

2.5 La Referencia 采纳《OpenAIRE 指南》 97

2.6 为评估出版商知识库服务提出准则 99

2.7 强化构建全球开放获取知识空间的目标 100

3 COAR 取得的合作与成果 102

3.1 主要知识库网络同意开展合作 102

3.2 可持续发展网络论坛的讨论 103

3.3 国际主要知识库组织同意采用通用指南 105

4 发展战略及计划 109

4.1 COAR 2016—2018 年发展战略 109

4.2 COAR 2016—2017 年工作计划 110

5 关于 COAR 114

5.1 关于 COAR 114

5.2 加入 COAR 的权益 114

5.3 加入 COAR 115

5.4 常见问题及解答 118

1 Current State of Repositories

1.1 Executive Summary

This briefing paper presents an overview of the international repository landscape. The paper has been produced by COAR on behalf of the Aligning Repository Networks Committee, a group of senior representatives from repository networks around the world. While principally intended for the Global Research Council (GRC), the paper has also been written with a broader audience in mind.

Over the last 20 years, open access repositories have been implemented around the world and are now fairly widespread across all regions. Repositories provide open access (OA) tore search publications and other materials and enable the local management and preservation of research outputs. They are a key infrastructure component supporting the growing number of open access policies and laws, the majority of which recommend or require deposit of articles into an OA repository.

OA repositories are increasingly connected through thematic, national and regional networks. In turn, these regional and national networks are further aligning their practices globally through the COAR Aligning Repository Networks Initiative, making their collections more valuable as it enables new services to be built on top of their aggregated contents. These services include tracking of research outputs for funders and research administrators, monitoring usage of publications, facilitating text and data mining, as well as peer review overlay services.

Crucially, repositories represent a distributed and participatory model in which institutions manage content locally, but contribute to the global knowledgebase through adoption of common, open standards. Distributed systems, such as a global network of repositories, have an inherent sustainability. They increase the resilience of infrastructure and foster social and institutional flexibility and innovation. They also enable the research community to regain some influence over the scholarly communication system.

With a growing number of funding agencies adopting open access and open science policies that rely on repository infrastructure for adherence, it is critical that the repository and funder communities forge closer ties and find mechanisms to engage in regular dialogue. In addition, given that there are different approaches across regions in terms of both policies and infrastructure, it is important that the diversity perspectives are considered as we collectively move forward. COAR, and its members and partners, welcome further discussion with the Global Research Council as we chart a course for a sustainable and dynamic future for scholarly communication.

1.2 Introduction

The trend towards greater openness is being driven by a growing recognition that our substantial global investments in research could have a much greater impact if they are widely shared and openly available to everyone. While this may not have been possible in the pre-internet world, the digital, networked environment has made this objective eminently achievable and within our grasp. Within this context, over the past 15 years open access repositories have become increasingly important components of the global research infrastructure.

Open access repositories play a variety of roles in the scholarly communication system, and these roles continue to expand and evolve. To date, their primary functions have been to provide visibility and open access to research outputs, with a focus on the journal literature, as well as to ensure archiving of this material over the long term. Much of the journal literature is currently only available through subscription and/or pay per view fees, creating a significant barrier to the widespread dissemination and use of this research knowledge. To improve the visibility and impact of their research, many funders have adopted policies that require open access to journal articles. Repositories are a key infrastructure component to support these policies. Indeed, the vast majority of open access policies and laws requiring or requesting authors to deposit articles into an open access repository.

Beyond providing access to research articles and other research outputs, open access repositories are developing other functionalities, especially as services are built on top of the network of repositories. These include providing funders and institutions with the ability to track funded research output across repositories; delivering usage data; hosting collections of academic journals; supporting text mining of content for new discoveries; and linking related content across the network. As open access expands to the broader concept of open science, including a wider range of content types, open access repositories will become indispensable for managing, tracking, and providing access to the full range of outputs produced through research.

The purpose of this briefing paper is to provide a concise and up-to-date overview of the state of open access repositories around the world. The paper was prepared for the Global Research Council by the Confederation of Open Access Repositories (COAR) on behalf of the COAR Aligning Repositories Network Committee, a group of senior representatives from repository networks around the world.

1.3 Repository Demographics

Repositories began to appear on the scholarly landscape in the late 1990's, but their real growth in numbers has occurred over that last ten years, mainly because of the availability of open source repository platforms and the establishment of the Open Archives Initiative Protocol for Metadata Harvesting (OAI-PMH), an interoperability protocol for exchanging information between repositories.

As of May 16, 2015, OpenDOAR, a service that monitors repositories, listed 2874 repositories worldwide. These repositories are distributed across the world, but are most predominant in Europe, Asia, and North America. This graph taken from OpenDOAR shows the current geographic distribution of repositories around the world.

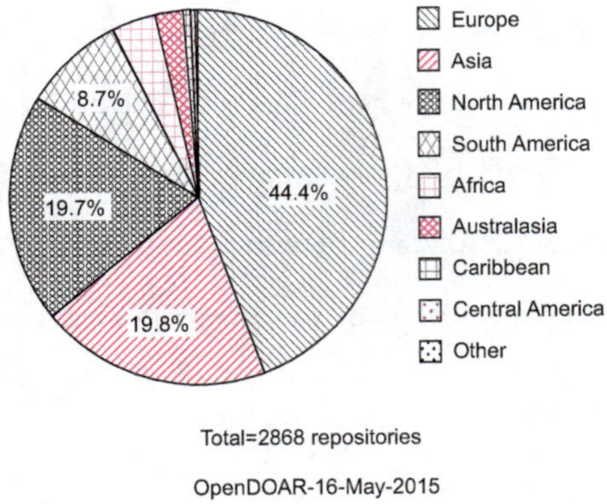

Fig. 1–1 OpenDOAR Graph of Repositories by Continent

The vast majority of repositories, just under 85%, are institutional repositories hosted and managed mainly by research institutions or universities, but there are also some very important and highly valued thematic repositories, including arXiv and PubMed Central, and journal repositories, including SciELO and Redalyc.

The repository landscape is quite diverse. Repositories vary greatly in their size service models, and the range of content types they collect. Most predominantly, repositories collect journal articles, e-theses and dissertations, and book chapters; but increasingly they are including research datasets, images and videos, and more.

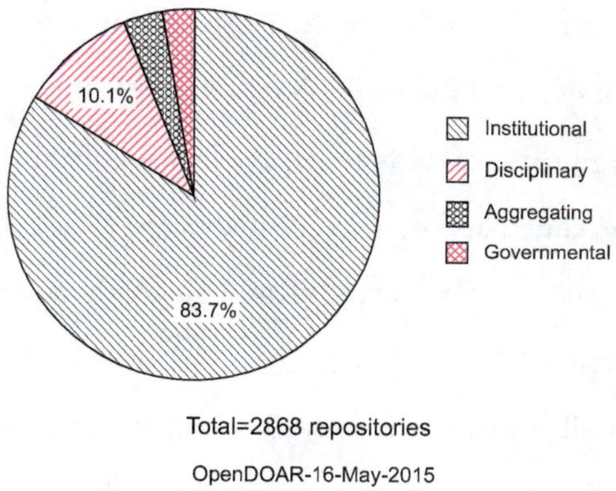

Fig. 1–2 OpenDOAR Graph of Open Access Repository Types

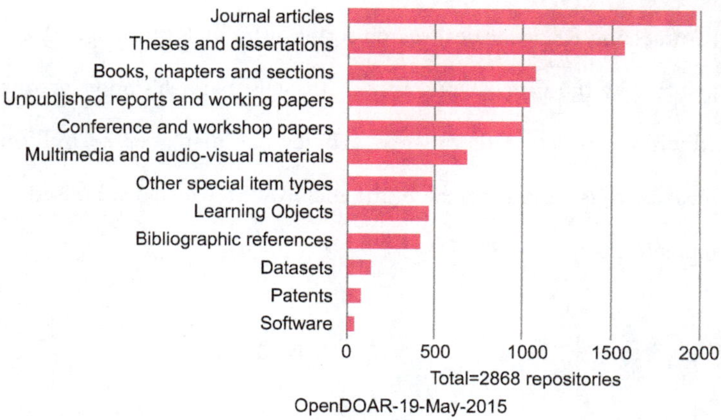

Fig. 1–3 OpenDOAR Graph of Most Frequent Content Types

It is difficult to assess the total volume of items in the repositories around the world, however, the BASE Search Engine, which aggregates records from (mainly) repositories around the world currently harvests over 72 million records from over 3000 sources, with approximately 17 million of them are records of journal articles.

Not all content in repositories is open access or full-text. A portion of the records in repositories either link out to published articles or have placed an embargo content on the full text item, usually because the publisher's policy requires this. The CORE (Connecting REpositories) search service, run by Knowledge Media institute at the Open University in the UK harvests only records which are attached to full-text articles has just over 24 million records in its central database, the majority of which are housed in repositories.

1.4 Regional Repository Networks

There is already significant repository infrastructure in many countries and regions of the world, which are connected through national and thematic networks. These networks have been created by governments in order to better track their research outputs, something that cannot be done by using traditional search engines or indexing services. In addition to national and thematic networks, several regional repository networks are being developed to connect repositories across national boundaries. These networks have evolved based on the unique local requirements and mandates, and are at different stages of development. Some networks are very organized, cohesive and have robust services, while others are in their developmental stages. Several of these networks are described below, but it should be noted that there are also repository systems in other regional and national contexts including Australia, India among others.

1.4.1 Africa

In Africa there has been a marked response to OA and a steady development of institutional repository initiatives particularly among universities and research institutions. According to OpenDOAR, there are currently 116 repositories from 21 African countries.

On the African continent, South Africa leads in terms of OA adoption among its public research and teaching institutions. In alignment to the GRC, the National Research Foundation (NRF) released an open access statement on January 30, 2015 that requires funded researchers to deposit their articles into an open access repository with an embargo period of no more that 12 months. A recent survey conducted in March 2015 by NRF showed that there are 27 repositories mostly hosted by universities in South Africa. The NRF has also developed a National ETD Portal, which harvest South African theses and dissertations for 17 out of 26 public universities. It is also assisting some local universities to develop their own repositories and three repositories were handed over to the recipient institutions in the past 2 years.

1.4.2 China

In China, both the Natural Science Foundation of China (NSFC) and Chinese Academy of Sciences (CAS) have issued policies on open access that mandate the deposit of peer reviewed drafts of papers funded by them, with an embargo of 12 months into a repository. To support this, CAS has built a Repository Grid that harvests records from 96 CAS affiliated institutional repositories.The grid currently indexes over 625,000 records from these repositories, which include 477,378 full text articles. The CAS network is extremely well used outside of CAS, with the collective content being downloaded over 11 million times and close to 5 million times from users outside China.

The Chinese Academic Library and Information System (CALIS), has also been promoting the development of IRs at academic institutions in China. Most recent data shows about 40 Chinese universities outside the CAS network have substantial repository operations. In addition, the Chinese Academy of Agricultural Sciences (CAAS) and Chinese Academy of Medical Sciences (CAMS) each have an institutional repository to provide access to articles and other research materials produced by their affiliated researchers.

1.4.3 Europe

Europe has a very robust repository landscape with about 44 percent (1275) of the world's repositories located on that continent. These repositories support a growing number of open access policies being adopted in various countries as well as the European Commission (EC). Since 2008, all EC grant agreements signed after August 2008 contained a clause requiring beneficiaries to deposit articles resulting from FP7 projects into a repository, and in the current funding program, Horizon 2020, the EC stipulates that all publications must be made open access.

Along with several very well developed national repository systems in countries like the United Kingdom, Portugal and Spain, the EC has been investing in a European-wide network, called OpenAIRE. OpenAIRE aggregates the research output of EC-funded projects and makes them available through a centralized portal. All member states are participating in OpenAIRE, as well as five associate countries, making a total of 33 countries involved in the project. OpenAIRE currently aggregates the metadata from over 590 repositories across Europe.

Although OpenAIRE's infrastructure is based on OA repositories, it has moved beyond a traditional publication aggregator. It currently aggregates 12.5 million publications and 7,000 datasets from 590 validated literature and data repositories. OpenAIRE links these records with funding information from the EC and other European Union national funders. On top of the validated, cleaned, and enriched metadata aggregated by OpenAIRE, they are also developing value-added services for a range of stakeholders, in particular research managers to help them monitoring their research output. In doing so, it is becoming a true research information system that demonstrates the value of open access and how this can be best implemented through community participation.

1.4.4 Japan

Japan has an extremely well developed repository network even in the absence of substantial funder open access policies. After some pioneering deployment of institutional repositories beginning in 2002, the Digital Repository Federation was formed by a group of interested universities in 2006 to lead efforts and bring together the Japanese institutional repository communities. Japan now has over 420 institutional repositories and is one of the countries with the greatest repository coverage. To support this repository network and ensure it is scalable, the National Institute of Informatics (NII) recently adopted the repository cloud service named JAIRO Cloud.

In 2013, Japan Science and Technology Agency, one of the national funding agencies, adopted an open access policy, making use of the system of repositories or open access journals. In 2014, Institutional Repository Promotion Committee was established for further cooperation with universities and NII and it is likely that open access activities will accelerate in Japan, with a recently published report, "Promoting Open Science in Japan" which strongly promotes open access.

1.4.5 Latin America

Traditionally, Latin America has been an open access continent, with an early and strong presence of regional Open Access journal repositories (SciELO and Redalyc), and in the past decade the development of institutional repositories and numerous open access policies by funders. Going beyond the adoption of policies, the governments of Argentina, Mexico and Peru have implemented laws that require all research output coming from government-funded research to be made freely available via a repository and discussions for new legislation in Venezuela and Brazil.

In order to support improved visibility of local scientific production through an affordable infrastructure, several Latin American governments formed La Referencia in 2012. La Referencia began as a project funded by the Inter-American Development Bank (IDB) between 2010 and 2013 and is now operated by RedCLARA, the organization that runs the high-speed network in Latin America. La Referencia maintains a centralized harvester, promotes common standards across Latin America and works at the strategic level to further promote open access. These services reflect the public policy agreements of the science and technology authorities in all 9 countries (Argentina, Brazil, El Salvador, Colombia, Chile, Ecuador, México, Perú, Venezuela) that were signed in November 2012 in Buenos Aires.

La Referencia currently harvests metadata from 8 national nodes aggregating from about 200 repositories, and representing over 800,000 full-text documents, which include journal articles, theses and dissertations, and research reports.

Latin America is one of the world's most progressive regions in terms of open access and adoption of sustainable, cooperative models for disseminating research; models that ensure that researchers and citizens have access to the results of research conducted in their region.

SciELO is a remarkable decentralized publishing platform harboring over 1,200 peer-reviewed journals from fifteen countries located in four continents-South America, Central-North America, Europe and Africa. Redalyc, based in Mexico, is another extraordinary system hosting almost 1,000 journals from fourteen Latin American countries plus Spain and Portugal. Governments around the world spend billions of dollars on infrastructure to support research excellence; platforms such as SciELO and Redalyc are extensions of this much larger investments in research. They reflect an enlightened understanding in Latin America that the wide dissemination of and access to research results is as important as the research itself. The rest of the world would do well to take note.

In a recent blog post, these two initiatives were discredited by Jeffrey Beall. In the post, Beall compared the two publishing platforms to favelas, resulting in a mean-spirited insult to both favela dwellers on the one hand, and SciELO and Redalyc on the other. Rather than maligning these initiatives, they should be held up as examples of best practice for the rest of the world.

Furthermore, just because some in North America do not know about SciELO and Redalyc does not render them irrelevant.

This is an extremely elitist and narrow view of the world. Although these platforms may not be well known in some places, SciELO and Redalyc do raise the visibility and accessibility of the journals they host, particularly with their local communities. If these journals were published by the big commercial publishers, the vast majority of researchers in Latin America would simply not have access to the articles in those journals. What value is visibility, if people cannot access the articles?

One of the United Nations Sustainable Development Goals, which were finalized on August 1, 2015, is to "Build resilient infrastructure, promote inclusive and sustainable industrialization and foster innovation". Both SciELO and Redalyc are excellent exemplars of this type of infrastructure. These types of networked meta-publishers allow for central governance of policies, procedures and controls, but are intentionally decentralized to support the development of local capacity and infrastructure ensuring greater sustainability and alignment with local policies and priorities. What Beall advocates for, namely to let powerful foreign players come in and take over local capacity building, is exactly the opposite of what sustainable development is about.

For these reasons, we believe that SciELO and Redalyc are very nice neighborhoods indeed!

1.4.6 North America

With a growing number of open access policies being passed by Canadian and US funding agencies, repositories have gained in importance and momentum in North America over the last several years. According to OpenDOAR, there are over 500 repositories in US and Canada, representing a very well developed repository landscape. In 2013, The US federal government directed each US Federal agency with over $100 million in annual conduct of research and development expenditures to develop a plan to support increased public access to the results of research funded by the Federal Government. The three Canadian research councils along with numerous private funder have also adopted open access policies, making the vast majority of researchers in this region regulated by open access requirements. As with most other regions, these policies are either neutral in terms of how researchers can adhere to the policy, or require specifically that researchers deposit into a repository.

In 2013, the SHARE project was launched to bring together information about publication output in this region. SHARE (SHared Access Research Ecosystem) is a joint effort supported by the Association of Research Libraries (ARL), the Association of American Universities (AAU), and the Association of Public and

Land-grant Universities (APLU) to strengthen efforts in North America to identify, discover, and track research outputs. The Center for Open Science has been SHARE's technical partner since 2014.

SHARE is creating an openly available data set about research activities across their lifecycle. Similar to OpenAIRE in Europe, SHARE aims to collect, connect, and enhance scholarly metadata for the purposes of better understanding and tracking research outputs. By creating an open data set, SHARE will provide opportunities for further innovation and analysis about research impact. SHARE's first service is called SHARENotify. Now in beta release, SHARE Notify takes metadata from a variety of digital repositories and generates a normalized feed of notifications.

1.4.7 Brazil

IBICT launches the new version of its portal of scientific publications.

Thousands of scientific publications produced in Brazil are more accessible to researchers and academics from around the world. All because it is already available the new version of the Brazilian Portal of Scientific Publications in Open Access, also known as http://oasisbr.ibict.br/.

The announcement of the launch of the new version was

made last July by the Brazilian Institute of Information in Science and Technology (IBICT), institution in charge of the site. The objective is to gather the Brazilian scientific publications in open access in one place, to facilitate the retrieval of these documents.

"Oasisbr is an integrated and adaptive research platform for mobile devices that concentrates the results of repositories, digital libraries of thesis and dissertations, and electronic journals of open access in Brazil. There are over six hundred forty collected sources, where we aggregate thesis, articles and many other scientific productions. Oasisbr also offers a set of statistics on collections and on the aggregate material, through which we can establish an overview of the Brazilian production", explains the coordinator of the Laboratory of Information Treatment and Dissemination of IBICT, Dr. Bianca Amaro.

To make the user experience even better, the page had significant changes in its interface. Another innovation is the upgrade of the system that makes the metadata harvesting of the participating institutions; this upgrade was a joint effort between engineers of IBICT and La Referencia who adapted the Vufind system. The platform also received components for collection and validation from La Referencia software, as well as a new OAI module that is able to export over a million registers.

In the opinion of Bianca Amaro, the cooperation with the Latin American network was one of the keys to the success of the project. "There was a strong synergy between our professionals, who in four months came to a modular and appropriate solution that supports the expansion of oasisbr to new sources of information and enhances the scope of the open access in Brazil. This fulfills our institutional goal to organize and disseminate the Brazilian scientific information, providing greater visibility to the national scientific production. We will continue inviting the Brazilian universities and research institutes to participate, to come and show to the world the results of its research. There is no doubt that the more we offer the research results, the faster we will advance in science."

Through oasisbr, it is possible to search and download approximately 1.2 million scientific publications in open access. There are over one million documents from Brazil and about 200,000 documents from Portugal, cause oasisbr also offers the productions of the Scientific Repository of Open Access of Portugal (RCAAP). The number makes the Brazilian portal the largest open access repository in Latin America.

It is also important to note that IBICT also adjusted for oasisbr important elements of its metadata, so that they are interoperable with international initiatives such as Driver and OpenAIRE, in Europe.

Get to know the new portal. Please visit: oasisbr.ibict.br.

1.5 Challenges and Opportunities

1.5.1 Alignment and Interoperability

It is clear that many regions around the world are investing in the development of repository networks. However, these networks have evolved in their own local contexts and differ in a number of ways. For example, there is significant diversity across regions in terms of implementation speed and availability of resources. Networks do not all share a common directive and have been deployed to support differing mandates and requirements. In addition, differences in language and geographic location present challenges to working together and identifying common approaches.

One of the major principles and aims reported in the Global Research Council's 2013 Action Plan is to create and interconnect repositories. The repository community, through COAR and other regional and national initiatives, has already made important strides towards this interconnection. While it would be impossible, and undesirable, to align networks across all areas, there are some important components where we should invest our efforts. Particularly urgent is to adopt standard practices for tracking and linking research publications with project, funders, and institutions. In addition, common approaches to measuring use of content, will allow us to reliably compare impact of research.

Open access repositories already adhere to the a minimum standard of interoperability through the Open Archives Initiative Protocol for Metadata Harvesting (OAI-PMH).However as repositories evolve, the community will need to adopt other agreed upon standards and practices that supports unified access to content across national borders. For example, if repositories use similar methods for recording funding information, measuring impact, and adhere to standard vocabularies, this will enable governments and funding agencies to better monitor the research outputs in which they invest.

In order to work towards greater alignment of repositories, COAR launched an initiative in March 2014 to bring together the major repository networks from around the world. The aim of this activity is to provide a mechanism whereby repository networks can promote interoperability and adopt common approaches to policies, practices and technologies. Through this initiative, repository networks are working in three areas to better align their activities:

technical and semantic interoperability, policies and advocacy, and service.

There are other benefits for the repository community in doing this. It enables networks to learn from each other, progressing the global community more quickly and leading to cost synergies by preventing duplication of work across networks. It is also a mechanism for repository initiatives to collectively express their perspectives to the international community.

In addition to aligning repository networks, repositories must be integrated and/or interoperable with other systems with which they overlap, including research administrative systems (CRIS), research data repositories, journal publishing platforms, indexing and abstracting services and search engines. This kind of integration is also happening via various forums including pilot projects at the institutional and network level, as well as increasing dialogue between the repository community and other important stakeholders. COAR has recently published a report, The "COAR Roadmap for Future Directions for Repository Interoperability" outlining priority areas for repository interoperability.

1.5.2 Balancing Global and Local Requirements

Many of the world's greatest challenges such as climate change, poverty, and health are global in nature and must be addressed in collaborative ways by researchers across regional and disciplinary boundaries. Conversely, there are important research problems, technical needs, and political and social environments in different regional/national and disciplinary contexts. As the distributed global network of repositories continues to evolve, we must find ways to support these two fundamental requirements.

Repositories are already well positioned to support local management of and access to research outcomes. By depositing articles and other content into local repositories in their own country, authors, who may have published their articles in international journals that are not accessible to individuals in their local environment, can ensure their work is accessible and used by important constituents.

On the other hand, as research becomes increasingly global, distributed and cross disciplinary, repository infrastructures also aim to belong to a global network where by researchers, regardless of location or disciplinary practice, to access research outputs worldwide. Striking the right balance between local needs and developing a truly global interconnection of repositories will be important.

1.5.3 Sustainability

The current publishing system, and consequently the flow of knowledge, remains under the control of the major publishers. This has created numerous disparities in the nature of scientific inquiry and the way findings are communicated, including barriers to access and newly emerging barriers to publishing that being introduced by the author or institution pays model.

Openness is about more than gaining access to knowledge. It is also about the being able to participate in the knowledge production process. As noted by the Global Research Council in the 2013 Action Plan towards Open Access to Publications, "in transitioning to open access, undue publication barriers must be avoided. It will be necessary to look for solutions that assist those authors in openly sharing their research results and thus making impact." While open access has made tremendous gains in terms of improving access to research publications, publishers are beginning to shift their business models from subscription to article processing charges (APCs). The consequence of this is to further marginalizing researchers at institutions in the developing world and smaller institutions who cannot pay the often large fees attached to them.

Investments in repositories allow the research community to take back some ownership of the scholarly communication system and manage it as a commons. They represent a distributed and participatory model whereby institutions manage content locally, but contribute to the global knowledgebase through adoption of common open standards. Distributed systems, such as a global network of repositories, have an inherent sustainability. They increase the resilience of infrastructure and foster social and institutional flexibility and innovation. These systems are managed by long-lived institutions such as universities, research centres, libraries, archives, and cultural institutions that have knowledge dissemination and stewardship at the core of their mandate.

1.5.4 Visibility

Open access repositories significantly raise the visibility, use, and citation of deposited articles. Numerous studies over the last 15 years have reported on the citation advantage of open access content in general. In terms of open access repositories, this also is true. For example, both arXiv and PubMed Central (PMC) are extremely well used. arXiv, which now provides access to over 1 million e-prints in Physics, Mathematics, Computer Science, Quantitative Biology, Quantitative Finance and Statistics reported about 1.5 million downloads per week in 2014. PMC is a free full-text archive of biomedical and life sciences journal literature that now contains over 3.4 million articles. While no public statistics are available, anecdotal evidence tells us that PMC is one of the most well used repositories in the world.

Usage of institutional repositories is also significant. The repository at MIT in the US(called DSpace@MIT) is one of the largest institutional repositories in the world, with a collection of more than 60,000 items. The repository receives, on average, more than 1 million downloads per month. Smaller repositories, such as the Nülan Repository from Universidad Nacional de Mar del Plata in Argentina, containing predominantly Spanish language articles, are very well used. In 2015, the repository which has just over 2,000 items, has had downloads of approximately 50,000 per month. Perhaps even more impressive are the individual download numbers for some of the articles in repositories. For example, the most downloaded item at the University of the West of England, Bristol has been downloaded over 65,000 times. Further technological and service development sin repositories, such as those described in the next section, will further increase the use and value of repositories in the scholarly community.

1.5.5 Value Added Services

In order to maintain their relevance, repositories must continue to evolve and expand their service offerings. Repository networks are increasingly used by governments, funders and institutions to monitor their investments in research. Networks, such as OpenAIRE in Europe, generate information for research administrators and funders to help them better understand and track their funded research outputs. Indeed, With over 5000 registered users, mainly research administrators, policy officers and principal investigators who use their services to analyze the impact of the research they fund, OpenAIRE has become are liable and trusted service for the EC and other policy makers.

Another emerging service for libraries is measuring usage. The repository community has already begun to incorporate usage statistics and other measures into their platforms. While the most widely recognized measures of impact are citation data and journal impact factors, new complementary measures are being introduced that may better reflect the real impact of research articles (and other research outputs). Many repository platforms are building in this type of functionality, which is highly valued by the authors who deposit into repositories.

The aggregation of repository content can offer the foundation for a whole host of text mining activities to be developed on top of the content. Text and data mining are becoming valuable analytical methods that allow researcher to discover interesting patterns and extract new knowledge from a corpus of content. Repository collections contain all kinds contain rich information, which could be further used, combined and analyzed through text mining techniques. A growing number of services are being developed to support these types of service. As text and data mining techniques in research are more widely adopted, repositories and the broader community will need to address some of the existing limitations that exist, including restrictive licenses imposed by publishers, copyright regimes, and technical limitations.

As we move from open access to journal articles, to a broader vision of open science, repositories are also expanding the scope of their services to support the collection and management of other content types. Research data, in particular is a growing concern for the research community. The current data centres around the world do not have the capacity to collect and provide access (where appropriate) to the huge volumes of research data produced by researchers around the world. Our investments in open access repository infrastructures should be extended to include all valuable research outputs including research data.

Repositories have not yet been incorporated into promotion and tenure system and, for the most part, do not yet contribute to a researcher's prestige. As such, they remain an afterthought in order to fulfill open access policy requirements or to give visibility and access to research output. In order to become more relevant and actively used by the research community, repositories can begin to develop quality assurance and peer review services that will bring the kind of value offered by journals. Some repositories are already adopting overlay services that support peer review on top of their collections. Epi science, for example, offers a technical platform for peer-review of content. It promotes the emergence of "epijournals", or journals that take their contents from preprints deposited in open archives such as arXiv or HAL, that have not been published elsewhere. This kind of approach could be also generalized to regional, or even a global network of repositories, eventually generating further value to the contents within the repositories.

1.6 Conclusions

Research is an international activity whereby progress builds on the reported results of colleagues from around the world. An unimpeded flow of knowledge is a critical factor for creating a strong research environment. The expanding distributed network of open access repositories collectively supported by long-lived institutions around the world represent a sustainable, equitable and cost effective way for the global research community to support the dissemination, sharing and reuse of research knowledge.

In the future, we envision a global network of repositories

that will act as the foundation for access, certification, quality assessment and further re-use of research outputs. As we move from open access to open science, repositories will become even more important components of the research landscape by supporting the dissemination and preservation of a wide range of outputs including research data. Furthermore, repositories are well positioned to support a new model of scholarly communication that reflects the continuous flow of knowledge as it evolves over time, rather than the static one currently in place.

With a growing number of funding agencies adopting open access and open science policies that rely on repository infrastructure for adherence, it is critical that the repository and funder communities forge closer ties and find mechanisms to engage in regular dialogue. In addition, given that there are different approaches across regions in terms of both policies and infrastructure, it is important that the diversity perspectives are considered as we collectively move forward. COAR, and its members and partners, welcome further discussion with the Global Research Council as we chart a course for a sustainable and dynamic future for scholarly communication.

2 Practice and Effort of COAR

2.1 COAR Published Interoperability Roadmap

Executive Summary

In the past few years, Open Access repositories and their associated services have become an important component of the global e-research infrastructure. Increasingly, repositories are also being integrated with other systems, such as research administrative systems and with research data repositories, with the aim of providing a more integrated and seamless suite of services to various communities. Repositories can also be connected into networks (e.g. at the national or regional level) to support unified access to an open, aggregated collection of scholarship and related materials that machines can mine enabling researchers to work with content in new ways and allowing funders and institutions to track research outputs.

Scholarly communication is undergoing fundamental changes, in particular with new requirements for open access to research outputs, new forms of peer-review, and alternative methods for measuring impact. In parallel, technical developments, especially in communication and interface technologies facilitate bidirectional data exchange across related applications and systems. The aim of this roadmap is to identify important trends and their associated action points in order for the repository community to determine priorities for further investments in interoperability.

The roadmap process began with the compilation of a comprehensive list of interoperability issues derived from a broad discussion in the information, publishing and repository community. An Expert Advisory Panel was then asked to rate each issue according to its level of complexity and temporal relevance (or timing). This report presents the results of this process, ranking the issues according to these dimensions. The table below presents the key aspects in a two-dimensional structure.

Table 2-1 Compilation Table of Interoperability Issues Related to Knowledge Base

	Short term	Medium term	Long term
Low Complexity	•Exposing Citation Formats •Supporting Data Export Functions •Supporting Author Identification Systems •Supporting Search Engine Optimization (SEO) •Exposing Publication Lists •Integrating Different Persistent Identifiers	•Exposing Persistent Identifiers •Supporting Authorization and Authentication •Improving Platform Stability •Supporting Institutional Services •Extending End-User Usability •Validating Repository Metadata •Supporting Visibility in Repository Registries •Supporting OAI Service Provider Usage •Integrating Availability Services •Supporting Embedding Services •Supporting Repository Ranking Systems	
Moderate Complexity	•Exposing Bibliometric Information	•Exposing Versioning Information •DeDuplication •Improving Registry Infrastructure •Monitoring Open Access Mandate Compliance	

(Continued)

	Short term	Medium term	Long term
High Complexity	•Exposing Usage Statistics •Supporting Additional Metadata Format(s)	•Publication of Research Data •Improving Metadata Quality (Data Curation) •Processing Related Full Text •Supporting Deposit Protocols •Defining Architectural Recommendations for Repositories and their Interoperability •Supporting Enhanced Publications	•Extending Usage of Visualization Tools •Supporting Linked (Open)Data •Extending/ Replacing Metadata Exposition Protocols •Handling of Complex/ Compound/ Nested Repository Objects •Supporting Long-term Preservation and Archiving

Through this process, nine issues have been identified as having immediate relevance, with varying levels of complexity. These issues can be viewed as represent the most pressing priorities for efforts around interoperability.

COAR is already working to advance interoperability in several of the priority areas including author identification systems, publication lists, persistent identifiers, usage statistics and bibliometric formats. In the fall of 2014, COAR launched an international working group with the major regional repository networks, as well as CASRAI and EuroCRIS to develop a blueprint for interoperability with the aim of developing a formal mechanism whereby these interoperability issues can be discussed and addressed.

Still, many challenges remain with improving interoperability. Many of the nine issues involve some level of standardization across vocabularies, metadata and indicators, both within the repository environment as well as with other systems. Interoperability in these areas, therefore, will require collaboration across countries and regions as well as with other systems developed by different communities. In order to achieve interoperability, the repository community must work with and engage in ongoing dialogue with these other communities. In addition, ensuring local implementation of guidelines and standards at the level of individual repositories is very difficult and often requires significant community outreach to raise awareness of the benefits of adopting standards. One strategy is to work with the repository platform developers to have the standards implemented into repository software systems. In parallel the available interfaces of repositories and the corresponding systems should be open to enable bi-directional communication and information channels in order to allow concrete system interoperability.

Despite the challenges, the success of future repository services depends on the seamless alignment of the diverse stakeholders at the local, i.e. institutional, national and international community level. COAR, with its vision of a global network of open access repositories, will continue to work towards greater interoperability both within the repository community as well as with other players in the scholarly communication system.

2.2 COAR Launches Draft "Resource Type" Vocabulary for Open Access Repositories

Open access repositories are evolving in terms of the roles they play and the attributes they aim to express in their records. Users want to know about additional metadata elements used for describing repository items, such as open access status, research funder, institutional affiliation, and so on. Given the truly international and collaborative nature of research, repositories must be connected and aligned around policy and practices, and standard controlled vocabularies are an extremely important aspect of this alignment. Through an active, international Editorial Board, COAR has begun to develop a series of controlled vocabularies for open access repositories.

The aim of this work is to build broad international consensus around vocabulary items for open access repositories. The Editorial Board has reviewed existing regional and topical metadata schemas including info: eu-repo (and OpenAIRE Guidelines), NISO Access and License Indicators, RIOXX, CERIF Semantic Vocabulary, CASRAI Dictionary and others. For each vocabulary element, a definition is provided, and the item has been translated into several languages that will be connected via linked data principles.

As a first step, the Editorial Board is making the first draft version controlled vocabulary, resource type, available for comment by the broader community. COAR invites you to provide feedback on the definition and the vocabulary terms that are provided in English and several other languages (Catalan, Chinese, French, Italian, Portuguese, Spanish, German, and Russian). All comments can be posted from the COAR website for consideration. The period for input will be two months from August 1 to October 1, 2015.

In the coming months the editorial board will be working on other vocabularies that will also be made available to the community for comment. This work contributes to COAR's broader objective to develop and maintain a set of international controlled vocabularies for open access repositories and ensure they are adopted widely.

The Resource Type Vocabulary Draft v.1.0 (July 2015) is available to read and for comment here (http://www.coar-repositories.org/activities/repository-interoperability/ig-controlled-vocabularies-for-repository-assets/deliverables/).

Support for this work has been provided by:

The COAR Controlled Vocabularies Editorial Board, COAR Interest Group Controlled Vocabularies for Repository Assets and ART (Artificial Intelligence Research) at University of Tor Vergata and the Food and Agriculture Organization of the United Nations that are providing the expertise and infrastructure for the creation and maintenance of the COAR Vocabularies, particularly as Linked Open Data.

2.3 COAR Joined Europe's OpenAIRE 2020 to Strengthen International Collaboration

Open access to research results has been recognized by

both funders and research institutions as a vital mechanism to spur innovation and to create a fair playing field. The European Commission has been at the forefront of open access and has adopted a comprehensive OA policy, requiring open access to all the articles resulting from its funded research. OpenAIRE 2020 is a funded project to develop and maintain the infrastructure to support the European Commission OA policy.

The Confederation of Open Access Repositories (COAR) is pleased to announce our participation in the OpenAIRE 2020, to work towards international alignment of repository networks, a key priority for COAR. COAR will lead the work package, "International Alignment", enabling us to further support work already underway at COAR to facilitate greater interoperability of the major repository networks: La Referencia, OpenAIRE, SHARE and others. In addition, COAR will continue to raise the visibility of repository networks in general as a sustainable option from providing open access to research outputs.

The project is vast and multi-faceted. It provides support for implementing open access at the local level through a network of National Open Access Desks (NOADs), it also addresses many other issues in the scholarly landscape including research into peer review, metrics, data-sharing legal considerations, and linked data.

Another aspect is support for the EC Open Research Data Pilot and providing relevant training for institutions which support researchers in sharing their data.

The project was launched in Athens, Greece in on January 28 & 29, 2015. More than 100 participants from over 50 partner institutions met in Athens to discuss work plans and ensure all participants are aware of the many different aspects of this large project. The kick-off was attended by Alberto Cabezas, Executive Secretary of La Referencia, the Latin-American initiative aggregating Open Access from nine countries, Margaret Kathleen Shearer, Executive Director, COAR and Katharina Mueller, Head of Office, COAR.

2.4 COAR @ IFLA World Library and Information Congress 2015

COAR Executive Director Margaret Kathleen Shearer attended the IFLA (International Federation of Library Associations and Institutions) meetings in Cape Town, South Africa that took place from August 15-21, 2015. The conference was attended by over 3000 delegates from around the world and was a good opportunity to network with other colleagues and continue to raise the visibility of COAR with the international library community.

Daisy Selematsela (member of the COAR Executive Board and Executive Director for Knowledge Management Corporate at National Research Foundation of South Africa) and Kathleen presented a joint paper about the COAR Aligning Repository Networks initiative and the South African open access policy and repository environment.

Kathleen also organized and moderated a panel about Libraries and Research Data that was co-sponsored by the Research Data Alliance (RDA). The panel discussed both regional and institutional perspectives for research data management in libraries. We had a number of COAR members participating in the session including Wolfram Horstmann (University of Goettingen), Zanele Mathe (Cape Penninsula University of Technology), and Daisy Selematsela (National Research Foundation of South Africa). A summary can be found in the handout that was prepared by Michael Witt at Purdue University for this session: "23 things libraries can do with research data."（https://rd-alliance.org/system/files/documents/23Things_Libraries_For_Data_RDA.pdf）

With colleagues from ARL (Association of Research Library) and CARL (Canadian Association of Research Libraries) Kathleen also presented papers about the SHARE project and Portage, a

Canadian library based network for research data management.

All presentations and papers form the IFLA conference will be made available soon.

2.5 La Referencia Adopted OpenAIRE Guidelines

COAR member La Referencia, the Latin America Open Access Repositories network, adopts major elements of OpenAIRE Guidelines to improve global interoperability. La Referencia is an initiative of public science and technology organizations of nine countries that offers a regional Open Access repository harvesting service.

In 2012, La Referencia chose to adopt Driver 2.0 guidelines and implementation mechanisms were agreed in mid-2012 for ten fields. Nearly three years later, the new La Referencia guidelines (Interoperable Metadata and Harvest Policies for La Referencia National Nodes) present and update the fields in a more detailed format, and provide recommendations for all the fields present in Driver. They also offer clarifications and changes derived from OpenAIRE (which currently maintains the guidelines) and define the main areas to work in future releases.

This effort began in mid-2014 as part of the work plan of La

Referencia, through RedCLARA, in the project OpenAIRE 2020. Launched in 2015, one of its objectives is to "create an international OA repository network to support global research and scholarly communication". Part of the OpenAIRE 2020 work package led by COAR, the aim is "to accelerate current activities in the area of interoperability by promoting alignment, and facilitating the exchange of good practices and the adoption of shared indicators, services and technologies across regional networks".

The main audiences of the guidelines document are the eight national nodes in La Referencia. It is probable that some of these alignments (depending on the field) will be reached at the level of transformation in the node of La Referencia and in the national node. At the same time, it presents a roadmap for the regional repositories to become interoperable internationally, while, allowing for the details and progress of implementation to be determined at the national level.

Central Elements

The biggest change, with full consensus among the representatives of La Referencia, is to make mandatory the "Rights" (dc: rights) field. It means that every document harvested by La Referencia should contain an explicit statement of access status based on the international vocabulary and our tradition in this area, and only articles assigned with either openAccess or embargoedAccess will be harvested by La Referencia. With regard to the licenses, the use of Creative Commons will be recommended.

openAccess (Open Access): Access without restrictions.

embargoedAccess (embargoed): The resource is restricted until is released in open access on a certain date.

The other fields, where applicable, that were agreed to are:

The fields Description, Subject, Language and Publisher will be changed from Recommended to Mandatory, if applicable.

The field Contributor will be included as recommended and the director or supervisor of a Thesis, will be mandatory, if applicable.

Relation, Coverage and Audience are Optional (As well as in Driver 2 and OpenAIRE).

And, the dc field: format will be recommended.

2.6 COAR Guidelines for Assessing Publisher Repository Services

A number of journal publishers have begun to offer services to the repository community. These services may differ according to publisher, however they generally involve the automated transfer of content (metadata and/or articles) into repositories.

COAR has adopted the following guidelines to help our members make informed decisions about such services. These guidelines are based on the underlying values and aims of the repository community, which are to provide open access to research outputs via a sustainable network of open access repositories.

COAR recommends that repositories only enter into publisher agreements that fulfill the following conditions:

(1) Services should include the transfer of both full text and metadata into the repository, and the transfer should occur either before or at the time of publication. Metadata linking from repositories to pay-walled, full text articles does not improve their accessibility and simply serves to drive traffic to the publishers'sites.

(2) Services should not impose embargo times of longer than 12 months (ideally, 6 months in the fields of Science, Technology, and Medicine) and existing publisher embargo periods should not be lengthened as a result of the adoption of the publishers' repository services.

Repositories are also encouraged to seek licenses that enable the re-use and full-text mining of content once embargo periods are over.

2.7 Reinforce the Aim to Develop a Global, Open Access Knowledge Commons

For a second year in a row, major open access repository networks have met to develop closer ties and further align their expanding repository networks. The meeting, organized by the Confederation of Open Access Repositories (COAR), was held on April 16, 2015 in Porto, Portugal and included representatives from Africa, Asia, Europe, Latin America, and North America. Amidst the intensifying global debate about the most sustainable ways to implement open access and research infrastructures, meeting participants reinforced their aim to foster solutions that reflect the diversity of approaches and capacities across different regions.

Repository networks are being developed around the world to support open access to research outputs. However, given the truly international and collaborative nature of research, these networks must be connected and aligned around issues such as policy, standards and services. At the meeting, delegates shared updates about their local networks. Many networks have evolved significantly over the last year and are now in a better position to collaborate more deeply. The group also reviewed the progress of the aligning repository networks activities since their meeting last year. Specific outcomes from the previous year's work include the publication of a joint statement against embargo periods, the launch of a technical working group seeking to harmonize open access elements and metadata schemas, and improved visibility of repository networks worldwide.

Participants also discussed priorities for further aligning their networks for the coming year. Activities will include closer cooperation around the development of guidelines and tools, and several bilateral collaborations between networks were suggested. In addition, it was agreed that a communication strategy be developed to continue to raise the visibility of repository networks as key infrastructure components. Support was also expressed for further engaging with policy makers and other stakeholders to ensure adoption of balanced open access policies.

COAR will work with the community to accomplish these activities in the coming year. A full list of participants and a report about the meeting will be available soon on the COAR website.

3 Cooperation and Achievement of COAR

3.1 Major Repository Networks Agree to Collaborate

On July 9 and 10, 2015, three major regional open access repository networks and aggregators (OpenAire, La Referencia, and SHARE), along with the Confederation of Open Access Repositories (COAR) and Center for Open Science (COS) met in Charlottesville, Virginia to discuss synergies and potential areas of collaboration.

Open access repositories are being adopted around the world to support and promote open science, a trend which maximizes our investments in research by making research outputs freely available to the world. Many of these repositories are connected via regional aggregators, which form sustainable, distributed repository networks that provide access to and preservation of the valuable content created through research and scholarship.

However, research is international, with researchers

collaborating across regions and continents to solve the world's most critical problems such as climate change, health, economics, and so on. The aim of this meeting was to ensure that regional repository networks are complementary, more integrated, and working together to create a seamless global network.

The meeting was very productive and revealed that the objectives, technologies and use cases for all three networks are highly aligned and that there is a strong willingness to work together. In particular, a number of specific areas were identified in which the networks commit to collaborate on:

Regular data exchange: Exchange data and develop agreements around jurisdictional harvesting and aggregation leading to greater coverage and efficiencies across regions.

Common metadata and vocabularies: Work towards consensus about key metadata elements and common vocabularies to express funders and institutional affiliations, open access status, and project IDs. This will contribute to the COAR-CASRAI work already underway aimed at developing common metadata elements and will support repository managers in better exposing their collections.

Common technological services: Assess the feasibility of adopting common broker/router technologies and other services.

Ongoing dialogue: Meet regularly to share approaches and

perspectives about technical and strategic challenges.

Over the next several weeks, the groups will develop a more detailed plan for achieving specific outcomes.

3.2 The Sustainable Development Goals E-forum Discussion

In September, the Sustainable Development Goals (SDG) e-forum discussion took place, jointly organized by the Food and Agriculture Organization of the United Nations (FAO), the International Federation of Library Associations and Institutions (IFLA) and COAR.

Over the 12 days of the forum, participants engaged in discussions about the role of access to information (and open access) in sustainable development. Participants contributed numerous examples, illustrations, and case studies that demonstrate that access to information and open access improves people's lives. Access to information and open access are cross-cutting issues that underpin most, likely all, of the SDG's and should be seen as a critical element for being able to achieve them. Strategies for promoting access to information are diverse and depend to a large extent on the local environment. Clearly, advocating with national governments takes time, but can be successful. Despite our differences, the whole community could benefit from greater information sharing about experiences and success stories. The archive of the discussion is available here: https://dgroups.org/fao/ciard-econsultation/sdgs-impact-access-information-societies/.

We had four presentations during the forum from: Stuart Hamilton, Jean Claude Guédon, Leslie Chan and Ellen Namhila. The recordings of all webinars are available on the FAO website here: http://aims.fao.org/capacity-development/webinars. We also received a short pre-recorded video that Ms. Amina Mohammed, Special Advisor of the Secretary-General on Post-2015 Development Planning entitled, "SDGs and Access to Information" https://www.youtube.com/watch?v=-6KMQV9VYg4&feature=youtu.be.

One of the important things that became clear in the e-forum was that open access repositories have a very important role to play in supporting sustainable development across the world. Not only do they provide access to knowledge and information published in (often) "out of reach" subscription-based journals, they also contribute to the development of local infrastructure and capacity building at institutions around the world. They ensure that local knowledge is preserved in the context where it was originally created. We should not underestimate the value of the distributed network we are building towards the creation of a more sustainable, open knowledge commons.

Yet there is still work to be done. The international journal system, in which most researchers highly desire to publish for the prestige, skews national research agendas towards issues of importance to Western Europe and North America. Several of the presenters talked about repositories as mechanisms for addressing this issue and creating a more equitable system. But this means expanding the role of repositories beyond just providing access, towards adopting value added services such as peer review.

In the coming months, we'd like to further expand on the ideas around open access repositories and such value added services in order to assess whether they are feasible and have merit to our community. Any further thoughts from the community on this are most welcome.

3.3 Major Repository Networks Agree to Adopt Common Guidelines

There is growing recognition worldwide that our substantial global investments in research have much greater impact if they are widely shared and openly available to everyone. La Referencia, OpenAIRE and COAR reaffirm their strong support for a shared vision of a global network of repositories as fundamental infrastructure for providing sustainable and open access to research outputs, ensuring that all researchers and citizens have access to the results of publicly funded research.

On November 25 and 26, 2015, representatives from La Referencia, OpenAIRE and COAR met in Rio de Janeiro to discuss the adoption of common metadata guidelines for repository networks and identify areas for further collaboration. The meeting was hosted by the Oswaldo Cruz Foundation (Fiocruz), along with Ibict (Instituto Brasileiro de Informação em Ciência e Tecnologia), and is part of the Aligning Repository Networks work being lead by COAR.

OpenAIRE and La Referencia represent two of the most advanced regional networks of open access repositories in the world. Closer collaboration between these two networks will enhance the usability and visibility of the collective content in the networks and enable the development of value added services across the two regions.

The three organizations therefore resolve to pursue their common vision through the following activities:

La Referencie and OpenAIRE will adopt common metadata practices, based on the current OpenAIRE guidelines and the vocabularies being developed in the context of COAR, for repository networks and develop these guidelines in collaboration.

COAR, La Referencia, and OpenAIRE will explore ways to build capacity for managing repositories and repository networks in Latin America, particularly in terms of the implementation of best practices.

Under the auspices of COAR, La Referencia, and OpenAIRE will continue to work with other national and regional networks to promote the vision of a global repository network and investigate common services in support of open access and open science.

La Referencia is the network of open access repositories from eight Latin American countries. It supports national open access strategies in Latin America through shared La referencia_OpenAIRE_Workshop2015_Mosaicostandards and a single discovery platform. La Referencia harvests scholarly articles and theses & dissertations from national nodes, which, in turn, harvest from repositories at universities and research institutions. This initiative is based on technical and organizational agreements between public science and technology organizations (National Ministries and Science & Technology Departments) with

RedCLARA.

OpenAIRE, funded by the European Commission under H2020, is the Open Access Infrastructure for Research in Europe, based on the network of open access repositories.

Specific agreements:

The national nodes of La Referencia will adopt the OpenAIRE Guidelines and, through La Referencia, participate in the development of the guidelines with OpenAIRE as they evolve in the future.

La Referencia will develop a strategy and launch communities of practice to facilitate sharing of expertise across participating countries and to support implementation of guidelines at local institutions.

La Referencia, OpenAIRE and COAR will partner to develop a blended learning course to build capacity in managing repositories in Latin America.

La Referencia and OpenAIRE will provide validators that will enable repositories to assess their level of compliance with the guidelines.

Participants:

Amaro, Bianca-Ibict, Brazil

Amórtegui, Miguel Ángel-RENATA, Colombia

Apollaro, Alberto-Mincyt, Argentina

Azrilevich, Paola-La Referencia/Mincyt, Argentina

Cabezas, Alberto-La Referencia, Chile

Granados, Diana-Colciencias, Colombia

Labbé, Carmen Gloria-COAR/RedCLARA, Chile

Matas, Lautaro-La Referencia, Argentina

Merino, Sonia Elsy-Min. de Educación, El Salvador

Muñoz, Patricia-CONACYT, Chile

Rasseli, Luiz Alberto-La Referencia, Brazil

Recavarren, Isabel-Concytec, Peru

Ribeiro, Washington-Ibict, Brazil

Rodrigues, Eloy-OpenAIRE/COAR/ Minho University, Portugal

Shearer, Kathleen-COAR, Canada

Siguencia, Josefina-CEDIA, Ecuador

4 Development Strategy and Plan

4.1 COAR Strategy 2016-2018

Vision

A sustainable, global knowledge commons based on a network of open access digital repositories.

Mission

To enhance the visibility and application of research outputs through a global network of open access repositories based on international collaboration and interoperability.

COAR Strategic Directions 2016-2018

To realize our mission and achieve this vision, COAR will focus on community, leadership and engagement at the international level.

Four strategic directions will guide COAR's activities:

(1) Promote the development of a sustainable, global network of open access repositories as key elements of international

research infrastructures in support of excellence in scholarship and education.

(2) Provide support for the OA repository community and build local capacity for the development and management of repositories and repository networks.

(3) Define and promote interoperability, common standards, and best practices for repositories, repository networks and with other related systems.

(4) Stimulate the development and adoption of value-added services for repositories and repository networks.

4.2 COAR Work Plan 2016-2017

For the years 2016-2017, COAR will deliver its strategic directions via the following work plan.

The work plan will be reviewed in early 2017 to ensure objectives and actions remain relevant in this rapidly evolving environment.

1. Promote the development of a sustainable, global network of open access repositories as key elements of international research infrastructures

Objective	Actions	Who
Promote the value of repository networks with important stakeholder communities	• Attend and present COAR work and vision at relevant conferences • Contribute to discussions on mailing lists and other online forums (when appropriate) • Participate in working groups and other related initiatives that reflect COAR's strategic objectives • Support regional repository networks in providing efficient and sustainable open access infrastructures for scientific publications, data and other resources • Work with open access groups and organizations to promote the COAR vision and objectives • Engage with other international organizations such as Global Research Council and UNESCO • Provide support for development and implementation of OA mandates, policies and laws	• Executive Director • Executive Board • COAR Subject Experts • Aligning Repository Networks Committee • COAR Office

Expand COAR membership	• Engage publicly on issues of importance to the repository community • Disseminate the work of COAR widely • Participate in activities of other organizations that will raise the profile of COAR • Consolidate and improve the COAR brand through targeted marketing and communications activities (internal and external) • Approach organizations to recruit new members • Develop a detailed plan that will clearly outline the activities devoted to growth of membership, fundraising, visibility, etc.	• Executive Director • COAR Office • Executive Board • COAR Members
Become a key stakeholder in relevant international e-infrastructure and scholarly communications	• Participate in governance of organizations and external consultations around e-infrastructure, open access and scholarly communications initiatives	• Executive Director • Executive Board

2. Provide support for the OA repository community and build capacity for the development and management of repositories and repository networks		
Objective	**Actions**	**Who**
Provide support and build capacity for the development and management of open access repositories and repository networks	• Plan events, workshops and seminars in conjunction with the General Assembly • Organize Virtual days about specific topics for COAR members • Participate in the Research Data Alliance and share relevant information with members • Develop training course(s) for repository managers with a special focus on developing countries • Initiate staff exchange program, using third-party funding • Launch a pilot project to partner COAR member institutions to support knowledge transfer, information sharing and staff exchanges	• Executive Director • Executive Board • COAR Subject Experts
Develop international best practices for repository management	• Investigate the potential for developing global quality indicators for managing open access repositories	• Executive Director • Executive Board • Possibly launch COAR group to undertake this activity

3. Define and promote interoperability, common standards, and best practices for repositories, repository networks and with other related systems

Objective	Actions	Who
Improve alignment between regional and national repository networks	• Develop and maintain a set of international controlled vocabularies for repositories • Discuss and develop consensus for adopting common vocabularies and metadata elements across networks via the COAR-CASRAI Working Group • Facilitate greater communication between repository networks as well as supporting bilateral activities between these networks	• COAR Controlled Vocabulary Interest Group/Editorial Board • Executive Director • Aligning Repository Networks Strategic Committee • COAR-CASRAI Working Group on Metadata Harmonization • Representatives from Individual Networks
Achieve greater interoperability between repositories and other systems	• Raise the visibility of the COAR Roadmap for Repository Interoperability • Work with other stakeholders and communities to harmonize metadata standards	• Executive Director • COAR Subject Experts • COAR Controlled Vocabulary Interest Group/Editorial Board
Improve the discoverability of repository content via search engines	• Produce guidelines for repositories for Google and Google scholar indexability for repositories	• Launch COAR group to undertake this activity

Work towards interoperability with research data management repositories and systems	• Participate in the Research Data Alliance (RDA) in the area of interoperability and work to develop interoperable metadata and vocabularies between publication and data repositories	• Executive Director • COAR Subject Experts

4. Stimulate the development and adoption of value-added services for repositories and repository networks

Objective	Actions	Who
Monitor trends in value added services	• Monitor and share with the COAR community new usage measures that can be applied in repositories	• COAR Usage Data and Beyond Interest Group
Promote sustainable strategies for populating repositories	• Collect, share and promote the implementation of open access clauses in publishers' licenses	• Executive Director • Licensing Task Group Force
Identify and implement new repository services	• Launch a pilot project to adopt peer review services layer on top of repository networks • Share information with COAR members about new services that are evolving for repositories • Develop a COAR Roadmap for Research Data Management (possibly in conjunction with RDA Libraries for Research Data Interest Group)	• Executive Director • Executive Board • COAR Subject Experts

Actively promote the development and adoption of next generation repositories	• Work with the repository platform developers and the repository community to identify and promote the adoption of new architectures, protocols, functionalities and features that reflect evolving technological environment	• Executive Director • Executive Board • Possibly launch a COAR group to undertake this activity

1 国际知识库现状

1.1 报告摘要

《促进开放科学和开放知识：知识库现状》报告概述了国际知识库现状。该报告由 COAR 代表联合知识库网络委员会撰写完成，其成员包括一批来自世界各地知识库网络的高级代表。虽然该报告主要是为全球研究理事会（Global Research Council，GRC）所做，但同时也考虑到了更广泛的受众。

过去 20 年里，开放获取知识库在全世界范围内得以实现，并在各个地区变得相当普遍。知识库提供对科研著作和其他材料的开放获取（Open Access，OA），同时实现对科研成果的本地管理和保存。它们是支持越来越多开放获取政策和法律的关键基础设施之一，大部分 OA 政策或法律建议或要求将文章存入 OA 知识库。

OA 知识库日益通过主题、国家和区域网络联系起来。反过来，这些区域和国家网络正在全球范围内通过 COAR 知识库合作网络计划进一步优化其实践，允许其在整个网络的整合内容之上构建新服务，使其资源集合更有价值。这些服务包括为资助者和科研管理者跟踪研究成果、监督出版物使用情况、促进文本与数据挖掘，以及虚拟整合期刊的同行评议服务。

关键是，知识库代表了一种分布式共享模式，即各机构在本地管理存储内容，但通过采用常见的开放标准为全球知识库做出贡献。诸如全球知识库网络等分布式系统具有内在的可持续性。它们将增加基础设施的弹性，培养社会和机构的灵活性与创造性。它们也将促使学术界重新获得在学术交流系统方面的影响力。

随着越来越多的资助机构采纳依赖知识库基础设施的开放获取和开放科学政策，在知识库和资助团体之间建立更为密切的关系并探求开展定期对话的机制很是关键。此外，鉴于各地区在政策和基础设施方面有着不同做法，那么在共同向前推进时，考虑到观念的多元化是很重要的。COAR 及其成员和合作伙伴制定了一条持续且动态的学术交流未来行动路线，欢迎与全球研究理事会做进一步讨论。

1.2　前言

更大的开放是一种发展趋势，因为人们日益认识到：如果对所有人提供广泛共享和开放获取，全球范围内的大量研究投入可以产生更大的影响力。在没有互联网的时代，这或许不可能，但数字化网络环境使得该目标非常切实可行，可以较好地准备和掌握。在该背景下，开放获取知识库在过去15年里已经逐渐成为全球科研基础设施的重要组成部分。

开放获取知识库在学术交流系统中扮演着各种各样的角色，这些角色将不断扩展和演化。到目前为止，它们的主要功能是提供对研究成果的可见性和开放获取，重点是期刊文章，以及确保其长期保存。大部分期刊文章目前只能通过订阅和（或）按次付费获得，给科研知识的广泛传播和使用造成了极大障碍。为提高研究的可见性和影响力，许多资助者已经实施要求期刊文章开放获取的政策。知识库是一项支持这项政策的关键基础设施。事实上，绝大部分的开放获取政策和法律都要求作者将文章存入开放获取知识库。

除了提供对学术论文和其他科研成果的获取以外，开放获取知识库正在开发其他功能，特别是构建在知识库网络之上的服务。其中，包括向资助者和机构提供跟踪各知识库中受资助科研成果的功能；传送使用数据；托管学术期刊集；支持内容文本挖掘以便有新发现；链接网络上的相关内容。随着开放获取扩展到更广义的开放科学，包括的内容类型更加广泛，开放获取知识库对于管理、跟踪和获取全部科研成果来说是必不可少的。

本报告的目的在于提供一份简明和最新的开放获取知识库世界状况概述。该报告由COAR代表知识库合作网络委员会为全球研究理事会撰写而成，其成员包括一批来自世界各地知识库网络的资深成员。

1.3 知识库统计特征

20 世纪 90 年代后期，学术界开始出现知识库，但其数量的实质性增长发生在那之后的 10 年内，主要是因为开源知识库平台的可用性和开放知识库元数据收割协议（Open Archives Initiative Protocol for Metadata Harvesting，OAI-PMH）的建立，OAI-PMH 是知识库之间交换信息的互操作协议。

截至 2015 年 5 月 16 日，监测知识库的服务门户 OpenDOAR 收录了全球 2874 个知识库。这些知识库分布在世界各地，但主要集中在欧洲、亚洲和北美洲。OpenDOAR 所给的图 1–1 展现出世界各地知识库的地理分布现状。

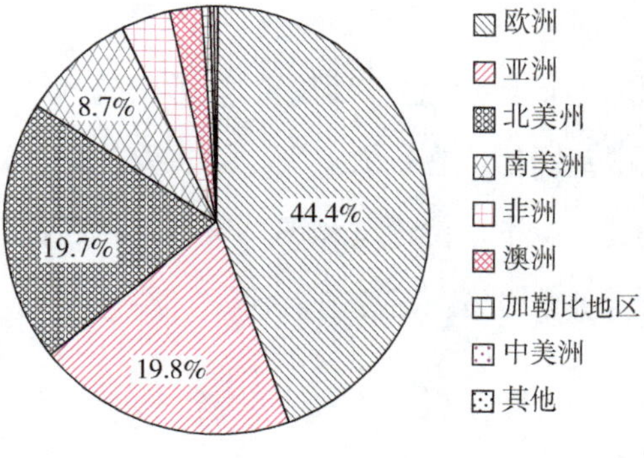

总数=2868个知识库

数据来源：DOAR（2015年5月16日）。

图 1–1 关于知识库各大洲分布的 OpenDOAR 图

绝大多数知识库（略低于85%）是由研究机构或高校建立和管理的机构知识库，但也存在一些非常重要和评价极高的专题知识库（包括arXiv、PubMed Central）和期刊知识库（包括SciELO、Redalyc）（图1–2）。

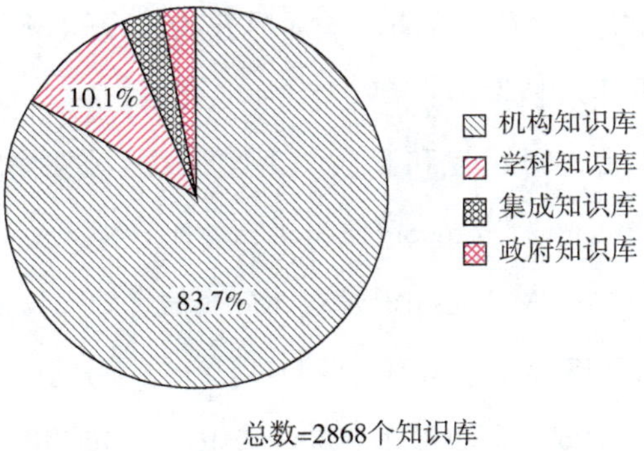

数据来源：DOAR（2015年5月16日）。

图1–2　关于开放获取知识库类型的OpenDOAR图

知识库趋于多元化。知识库的服务模式、规模和所收录的内容类型范围都存在很大差别。最主要的是，知识库收录了期刊论文、电子学位论文和图书章节，但它们逐渐开始涵盖更多的科研数据集、图片和视频等（图1–3）。

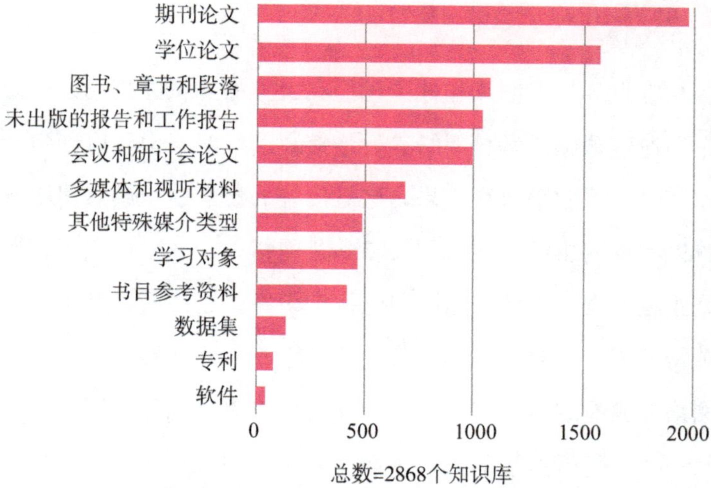

数据来源：DOAR（2015年5月19日）。

图 1–3 关于最常见内容类型的 OpenDOAR 图

很难评估世界各地的知识库条目总量，然而，从世界各地（主要）知识库整合记录的 BASE 搜索引擎已经收集到来自 3000 多个数据源超过 7200 万条记录，其中大约 1700 万条是期刊论文记录。

并非所有的知识库内容都允许开放获取或全文获取。知识库中的部分记录是链接到出版商网站的文章，或者为全文设置了开放获取时滞期，这通常是根据出版商的政策要求。英国开放大学的知识媒体研究的连接信息库（Connecting Repositories）收集到 2400 多万条附有全文的记录，其中大多数被存放到各个知识库中。

1.4 区域知识库网络

在世界许多国家和地区已经有大型的知识库基础设施，它们通过国家或学科网络进行连接。这些网络由政府创建，旨在更好地跟踪研究成果，这是传统的搜索引擎或索引服务难以实现的事情。除了国家和学科网络，一些区域知识库网络正在开发，以便跨越国界连接知识库。这些网络基于当地独特的需求和要求逐步演化，并处于不同的发展阶段。一些网络非常有组织、有凝聚力，并且可以提供稳健的服务，而另一些正处于发展阶段。下面将介绍其中几个网络，但需要指出的是，其他地区和国家也存在知识库体系，包括澳大利亚、印度等。

1.4.1 非洲

非洲对 OA 的响应明显，尤其是在高校和科研机构中，机构知识库计划稳步发展。根据 OpenDOAR 所示，它目前收录有来自 21 个非洲国家的 116 个知识库。

在非洲大陆，南非率先在其公共研究和教学机构中采纳 OA。与 GRC 保持一致，国家研究基金会（National Research Foundation，NRF）于 2015 年 1 月 30 日发布了开放获取声明，要求所资助的研究人员在不超过 12 个月的时滞期内将其文章存入开放获取知识库。由 NRF 于 2015 年 3 月开展的一项最新调查显示，有 27 个知识库主要由南非高校主管。NRF 也创建了国家电子学位论文门户，囊括了南非26所公立大学中的17所。它还帮助地方大学发展自己的知识库，并且在过去的2年里将3个知识库移交给接收机构。

1.4.2 中国

在中国，国家自然科学基金委员会（Natural Science Foundation of China，NSFC）和中国科学院（Chinese Academy of Sciences，CAS）发布了开放获取政策，要求在不超过12个月的时滞期内将其资助的同行评议论文审定稿存入知识库。为支持该政策，CAS建立知识库网格，收集来自96个CAS附属机构的知识库的记录。目前该网格从这些知识库中索引到超过625 000条记录，其中包括477 378篇文章全文。CAS网格在CAS之外得到充分利用，收集到的内容被下载超过1100万次，其中被国外用户下载近500万次。

中国高校图书馆联盟（Chinese Academic Library and Information System，CALIS）促进了IRs在中国学术机构中的发展。有关数据显示，除CAS网络以外，有约40个中国高校实施了大量知识库运作。此外，中国农业科学院（Chinese Academy of Agricultural Sciences，CAAS）和中国医学科学院（Chinese Academy of Medical Sciences，CAMS）各拥有一个机构知识库，能够提供其研究人员创作的文章和其他研究材料的获取。

1.4.3 欧洲

欧洲的知识库发展非常健壮，拥有世界上约 44%（1275个）的知识库。这些知识库支持越来越多被各国及欧盟委员会（European Commission，EC）采用的开放获取政策。2008年 8 月后签署的所有 EC 拨款协议包括一则条款，要求受资助人将FP7(欧盟第七框架计划，是欧盟主要的科研资助计划)资助项目产出的文章存入知识库，并且 EC 规定当前研究计划 Horizon 2020 中资助项目的所有出版物必须开放获取。

连同一些发展良好的国家知识库体系，如英国、葡萄牙、西班牙等，EC 现在投资于欧洲范围内的知识库网络OpenAIRE。OpenAIRE 聚集了 EC 所资助项目的研究成果，使其通过一个集中门户公开可用。所有成员国及 5 个联系国都加入了 OpenAIRE，因而共有 33 个国家参与该项目。目前OpenAIRE 整合了来自 590 多个欧洲知识库的元数据。

尽管 OpenAIRE 的基础设施是基于 OA 知识库，但它已经超越了传统的出版物汇总模式。目前，OpenAIRE 已经从 590 个有效的文献和数据知识库中整合出 1250 万种出版物和 7000 个数据集。OpenAIRE 将这些记录与 EC 和其他欧盟资助者的资助信息链接。OpenAIRE 在对整合来的元数据进行验证、清洗和丰富的基础上，还将为利益相关者，特别是科研管理者，开发增值服务来帮助他们监测其科研成果。这样，它将成为一种真正的科研信息系统，展现开放获取的价值和如何通过社区参与得以最佳实现。

1.4.4 日本

即使尚无实质性的资助者开放获取政策，日本依然拥有非常发达的知识库网络。自 2002 年一些机构知识库率先开展部署后，2006 年，一群感兴趣的高校组成了数字知识库联盟来试图将日本机构知识库团体汇聚在一起。现在日本有超过 420 个机构知识库，是最大的知识库拥有国之一。为支持该知识库网络并确保其可扩展，国立情报学研究所（National Institute of Informatics，NII）最近采用了名为日本机构知识库在线（Japanese Institutional Repository Online，JAIRO，网址为 http://jairo.nii.ac.jp）云的知识库云服务。

2013 年，为利用知识库系统或开放获取期刊，国家资助机构之一的日本科学技术振兴机构颁布了开放获取政策。2014 年，为进一步加强与高校和 NII 之间的合作，机构知识库促进委员会成立。最近发表的一份以“促进日本的开放科学”为题的报告大力推动了开放获取，将加快日本的开放获取进程。

1.4.5 拉丁美洲

传统上，拉丁美洲是一个开放的大陆，较早出现强力的区域开放获取知识库（如 SciELO 和 Redalyc），并且在过去 10 年里不断发展，资助者也制定了大量开放获取政策。在制定 OA 政策的基础上向前一步，阿根廷、墨西哥和秘鲁政府已经通过了要求通过知识库免费获取所有政府资助的研究成果的法律，委内瑞拉和巴西也开展了有关新法规的讨论。

为通过合理的基础设施支持提高本地科学成果的可见性，一些拉美国家在2012年组成了La Referencia。La Referencia起源于2010—2013年由美洲开发银行（Inter-American Development Bank，IDB）资助的一个项目，该项目目前由RedCLARA运作（RedCLARA是一个在拉丁美洲运行高速网络的组织）。La Referencia维护着一个中央收割器，推动整个拉丁美洲采用通用标准，并致力于在战略层面进一步促进开放获取。这些服务反映了9个国家（包括阿根廷、巴西、萨尔瓦多、哥伦比亚、智利、厄瓜多尔、墨西哥、秘鲁、委内瑞拉）的科学与技术部门于2012年11月在布宜诺斯艾利斯签署的公共政策协议要求。

La Referencia目前收集了来自8个国家的约200个知识库的元数据，包含了80多万篇全文文档，包括期刊论文、学位论文和研究报告。

就开放获取及采用连续合作的传播研究模式而言，拉丁美洲是世界上最先进的地区之一，拉丁美洲的开放获取模式确保了研究人员和市民在自己的地区可以获取研究结果。

科技电子在线图书馆（Scientific Electronic Library Online，SciELO）是一个出色的分布式出版平台，收录了来自南美洲、北美洲中部、欧洲和非洲15个国家超过1200种同行评审期刊。Redalyc，总部设在墨西哥，是另外一个卓越的系统，这一系统收录了来自 14 个拉丁美洲国家及西班牙、葡萄牙的近 1000 种期刊。世界各国政府在基础设施上都花费数十亿美元来支持研究实力，SciELO、Redalyc 平台，就是政府在学术研究上做出很大投入的例证。这些举措都反映了拉丁美洲在学术的广泛传播、获取跟学术本身同样重要这一点上已经有了清晰的认识。世界其他各国也应如此。

最近的一篇博客提到，Jeffrey Beall 对这 2 项平台的倡议持怀疑态度。在陈述中，Beall 将这 2 个出版平台比作贫民窟，一方面是对贫民窟居民的侮辱，另一方面也侮辱了 SciELO 和 Redalyc 平台。与其诋毁这 2 项倡议，不如让这 2 项倡议成为对世界其他地区最好的范例。

此外，不能因为一些北美的人不知道 SciELO 和 Redalyc 平台就因此说明它们不相干。这是一个极度高傲的、狭隘的世界观。尽管，这些平台可能在一些地方不出名，但是 SciELO 和 Redalyc 确实提高了它们收录期刊的可见性和可获得性，尤其是在当地的团体中。如果这些期刊被大的商业出版商出版，众多拉丁美洲研究人员将不能在这些期刊中获取文献。如果人们没办法获取文献，文献的可视化又有什么价值呢?

2015 年 8 月 1 日确定的国际可持续发展的一个目标是“建立弹性的基础设施，促进包容性和可持续的产业化和促进创新”。SciELO 和 Redalyc 就是这种基础设施的优秀典范。这些网络出版商允许政策、程序和控制的集中管理，但是有意分散，以支持当地的发展能力和基础设施，确保与当地政策和优先权保持更优质的持续合作。Beall 支持引入外国人来掌管当地的能力建设，而这恰恰是与可持续发展相对立的。

正是这些原因，我们相信 SciELO 和 Redalyc 确实是很好的参照！

1.4.6 北美洲

随着加拿大和美国资助机构通过越来越多的开放获取政策，过去几年里，知识库在北美洲的重要性增加并呈现良好发展势头。根据 OpenDOAR 所示，美国和加拿大有 500 多个知识库，展现出良好的知识库发展前景。2013 年，美国联邦政府要求每个研发资金支出超过 1 亿美元的联邦机构制订计划来支持公开获取联邦政府所资助研究的成果。加拿大三大研究委员会及众多私人资助者也实行开放获取政策，使该地区的绝大多数研究人员受到开放获取要求的约束。与其他大多数地区一样，这些政策要么允许研究人员选择开放获取的途径，要么明确要求研究人员将其成果存入知识库。

2013 年，SHARE（SHared Access Research Ecosystem）项目启动，以汇集该地区的出版物产出信息。SHARE 是研究图书馆协会（Association of Research Libraries，ARL）、美国大学协会（Association of American Universities，AAU）和美国公立与赠地大学协会（Association of Public and Land-grant

Universities，APLU）的共同努力成果，旨在更快努力识别、发现和跟踪北美的研究成果。开放科学中心自 2014 年以来一直是 SHARE 的技术合作伙伴。

SHARE 正在创建一项关于研究活动整个生命周期的公开可用的数据集合。与欧洲的 OpenAIRE 类似，SHARE 旨在收集、连接和加强学术元数据以便更好地理解和跟踪研究成果。通过创建开放数据集，SHARE 将为创新和学术影响力分析提供机遇。SHARE 的第一个服务被称为 SHARE Notify。在测试版本中，SHARE Notity 从各个数字化知识库中获取元数据并生成规范化的记录。

1.4.7 巴西

巴西科学技术信息研究所（Brazilian Institute of Information in Science and Technology，Instituto Brasileiro de Informação em Ciência e Tecnologia，简称 IBICT，网址为 http://www.ibict.br/）发布其新版科学出版物门户网站。

巴西产出的成千上万本科学出版物将更容易地被来自世界各地的研究人员和学者获取，一切都是因为这些成果已经被新版本的巴西开放获取科学出版物门户网站 oasisbr 收录。IBICT 在 2014 年 7 月宣布推出新版本。网站目标是将巴西可开放获取的科学出版物聚集起来，从而方便检索这些文件。

Bianca Amaro 博士在解释 IBICT 信息处理和传播实验室的协调作用时谈道：“oasisbr 是一个集成式自适应移动设备

研究平台，集中了巴西的成果知识库、数字图书馆学位论文和开放获取电子期刊。它拥有超过 640 种资料收集来源，汇集了学位论文、期刊文献和许多其他科研产出。oasisbr 还提供了一组关于收藏品和聚集材料的统计数据，通过这些我们可以大致了解巴西的科研产出情况。”

为了让用户获得更好的体验，网页界面发生了显著变化。另一创新之处是对负责参与机构元数据收割的系统进行升级，这一升级是 IBICT 工程师和改写 Vufind 系统的 La Referencia 的共同努力成果。该平台还采纳了来自 La Referencia 软件的收集和验证组件，以及一个能输出超过 100 万个注册用户的新的 OAI 模块。

Bianca Amaro 认为，与拉丁美洲网络之间的合作是项目成功的关键之一。“我们的专业人员之间存在很强的协同作用，他们在 4 个月内提出了一套模块化的、适当的解决方案，支持 oasisbr 扩大新的信息来源，提高了巴西开放获取的范围。这满足了组织与传播巴西科研信息的机构目标，为国家科研生产提供了更好的视野。我们将继续邀请巴西高校和研究机构参与进来，向世界展示其科研成果。毫无疑问，我们提供的科研成果越多，取得的科学进步就越快。”

借助 oasisbr，可以搜索和下载约 120 万本开放获取科学出版物。其中包括来自巴西的 100 多万个文件和来自葡萄牙的约 20 万个文件，使得 oasisbr 能够提供葡萄牙开放获取科学知识库（Scientific Repository of Open Access of Portugal，Repositório CientiPico de Acesso Aberto de Portugal，RCAAP，网址为 https://www.rcaap.pt/）的产品。这一数字使巴西门户网站成为拉丁美洲最大的开放获取知识库。

还要特别注意的是，IBICT 对 oasisbr 元数据的重要元素进行了调整，以便可以与欧洲的国际计划进行互操作，如 Driver 和 OpenAIRE。

想要了解新的门户网站，请访问：oasisbr.ibict.br。

1.5 挑战和机遇

1.5.1 一致性和互操作性

很明显，世界许多地区正在投资于知识库网络的发展。然而，这些网络的自身环境不断演化，并在很多方面存在差异。例如，各地区在实现速度和资源的可用性方面存在显著差异。并不是所有的网络都遵守一个通用的政策指令，这些网络在部署中也用于支持不同的要求和需求。此外，语言和地理位置的差异向携手合作和确定通用方法提出了挑战。

全球研究理事会 2013 年行动计划的主要原则和目标之一是创建知识库并使其互连。通过 COAR 和其他区域与国家性的举措，知识库团体已经在互连方面取得长足进展。尽管整合所有区域内的网络是不可能并且不可取的，但有一些重要环节需要我们投入大量精力。最为迫切的是采用标准规范来跟踪科研著作和将其与项目、资助者及机构相连接。此外，采用通用的方法来测量内容的利用情况将使我们能够可靠地比较研究的影响力。

开放获取知识库通过 OAI-PMH 协议来遵循最低的互操作标准。然而，随着知识库不断发展，该领域需要采取其他相互认同的标准和做法来支持跨国界内容的统一访问。例如，一旦知识库使用相似的方法来记录资助信息、衡量影响力并遵循标准词汇表，这将促使政府和资助机构能够更好地监测他们投资的研究成果。

为争取知识库之间形成更强的一致性，COAR 在 2014 年 3 月推出了一项计划，汇集来自世界各地的主要知识库网络。该活动旨在提供一种机制，知识库网络能够借此提升互操作性和采用有关政策、实践和技术方面的常见做法。通过这一举措，知识库网络可以在 3 个方面更好地调整其活动：技术和语义互操作；政策和宣传；服务。

知识库团体这样做还存在其他益处。它使得网络之间能够互相学习，更快地推动全球社会进步，并通过防止重复性工作实现成本协同效益。它也是知识库计划共同向国际社会表达自身观点的一种机制。

除整合知识库网络之外，知识库必须与其发生交集的其他系统集成或实现互操作，包括研究管理系统（如 CRIS）、科研数据知识库、期刊出版平台、索引与文摘服务及搜索引擎。通过各种平台也在实现这种集成，其中包括机构和网络层面的试点项目，加强了知识库团体和其他重要利益相关者之间的对话。COAR 最近发表了一份题为《COAR 关于知识库互操作性的未来发展路线图》的报告，概述了知识库互操作性的重点领域。

1.5.2 平衡全球和本地需求

世界面临的许多最重大挑战（诸如气候变化、贫穷和健康）都是全球性的，必须由各地区和各学科研究人员共同来解决。相反，在不同地区 / 国家和学科背景下存在一些重要的研究问题、技术需求及政治与社会环境。随着分布式全球知识库网络不断发展，我们必须找到支持这 2 种基本需求的方式。

一方面，知识库能够支持研究成果的本地管理和获取。对于那些把论文发表在本地难以获取的国际期刊上的作者，通过把文章和其他内容存储到自己国家的本地知识库，能够确保其工作成果是可获取的并被重要用户所用。

另一方面，随着研究日益全球化、分布式且跨学科发展，知识库基础设施旨在纳入一个全球网络，无论地理位置或学科实际情况，研究人员借此能在全球范围内获取科研成果。在本地需求和实现全球知识库互联之间找到平衡是非常重要的。

1.5.3 可持续性

当前的出版系统和知识流动仍然受制于主要出版商，这给科学探究和研究交流的方式造成了众多的不平等，包括访问壁垒及由作者或机构付费模式产生的新兴的出版障碍。

开放不仅仅意味着获取知识，也意味着人们能够参与到知识的生产过程。正如全球研究理事会在面向出版物开放获取的2013年行动计划中所提到的："在向开放获取过渡期间，必须避免不适当的出版障碍。有必要寻找解决方案，帮助作者们公开共享研究成果并产生影响。"开放获取在改善科研出版物获取方面取得了巨大进展，出版商的商业模式开始从订阅向论文处理费用（Article Processing Charges）转变。这样做的后果是进一步边缘化发展中国家机构和小型机构的研究人员，因为他们无法支付巨额费用。

投资知识库使学术界能够收回对学术交流系统的部分所有权并共同对其进行管理。知识库代表着一种分布式和参与式的模式，机构借此能够管理本地内容，并通过采用通用开放标准为全球知识库做出贡献。诸如全球知识库网络等分布式系统具有内在可持续性。它们能增加基础设施的弹性，培养社会和机构的灵活性和创新性。这些系统由长期存在的机构进行管理，如高校、研究中心、图书馆、档案馆和文化机构，其核心使命在于对知识进行传播和管理。

1.5.4 可见性

开放获取知识库明显改善了所存储文章的可见性、使用和引用情况。过去15年里众多研究报道了开放获取内容的引用优势。就开放获取知识库而言，这也是真实的。例如，arXiv和公共医学中心（PubMed Central，PMC）得到了非常广泛的应用。arXiv现在提供物理、数学、计算机科学、计量生物学、计量金融学和统计学方面的100多万份电子预印本，报道称2014年拥有每周约150万次的下载量。PMC是一个免费存储生物医学和生命科学领域期刊文章的全文存储库，目前包含340多万篇文章。虽然并没有公开可用的统计数据，但事实告诉我们，PMC是世界上使用最广泛的知识库之一。

机构知识库的利用也有着重要意义。美国麻省理工学院知识库（称为DSpace@MIT）是世界上最大的机构知识库之一，拥有60 000多份作品。知识库平均每月有超过100万次下载。小型知识库，如主要包含西班牙语文章的阿根廷拉普拉塔国立大学的Nülan知识库，也被广泛利用。2015年，拥有2000多份作品的该知识库每月下载量达近50 000次。不过令人更为惊叹的是，知识库中某些文章的单个下载量，例如，西英格兰大学的一份作品下载量最大，已超过65 000次。下面即将介绍的知识库技术和服务的进一步发展，将进一步提高知识库在学术界的利用率和价值。

1.5.5 增值服务

为维持其关联性，知识库必须持续发展，并扩大服务提供范围。政府、资助者和机构越来越多地采用知识库网络来监测其研发投资。诸如欧洲的 OpenAIRE 等网络为科研管理者和资助者生成信息以帮助其更好地理解和跟踪所资助的研究成果。事实上，OpenAIRE 拥有 5000 多个利用其服务分析所资助研究影响力的注册用户，主要是科研管理者、政府官员和项目负责人。对 EC 和其他决策者而言，OpenAIRE 已成为一种可靠和值得信赖的服务。

另一种新兴的图书馆服务是科研成果利用情况测度。知识库团体已开始将利用情况的统计数据和其他测度指标纳入其平台。虽然被广泛认可的影响力测度指标是引文数据和期刊影响因子，但引入新的补充测度指标可以更好地反映学术论文（和其他研究成果）的实际影响力。该功能受到向知识库存储文章的作者的高度评价，许多知识库平台正在构建这种功能类型。

知识库内容整合能为基于内容的文本挖掘打下基础。文本和数据挖掘逐渐成为有价值的分析方法，允许研究人员从语料库中寻找有趣的模式并提取新知识。知识库集合包括各种丰富的信息，通过文本挖掘技术对其做进一步利用、组合和分析。越来越多的服务被开发以支持这些服务类型。随着更为普遍地在研究中采用文本和数据挖掘技术，知识库和更为广泛的团体需要解决一些现存限制，包括出版商强加的许可限制、版权制度和技术限制。

当我们从期刊文章开放获取向更广泛的开放科学转移

时，知识库也扩大其服务范围来支持对其他类型内容的收集和管理。科研数据正受到学术界的日益关注。目前世界各地的数据中心还没有能力收集并提供对全球研究人员产生的大量科研数据的获取。我们在开放获取知识库基础设施方面的投资应该扩展到所有有价值的科研成果上，其中包括科研数据。

知识库（内容的存缴和使用情况）尚未纳入晋升和终身聘任系统，在大多数情况下，还未对研究人员的声望做出贡献。因此，在满足开放获取政策需求或给予研究成果可见性和可用性，它们仍然属于补救措施。为变得更相关及被学术界积极利用，知识库开始构建质量保证和同行评议服务，将带来期刊所提供的类似价值。一些知识库已经采用支持基于其资源集合进行同行评议的增值服务。例如，Eriscience 为同行评议提供了技术平台。它可以催生新的“epijournals”或从存储在诸如 arXiv 或 HAL 等开放知识库的预印本中抽取内容的期刊，这些预印本并未在其他地方进行发表。这种方式可以被推广到区域乃至全球知识库网络中，最终让知识库内容进一步产生价值。

1.6 报告结论

该研究是一项国际活动，借此能够在世界各地同行的报告成果基础上取得进步。畅通的知识流动是搭建强大研究环境的关键因素。受到世界各地历史悠久的机构支持的、不断扩展的分布式开放获取知识库网络，代表了一种可持续的、公平的和经济有效的方式，使全球学术界支持研究知识的传播、共享和重用。

在将来，我们构思了一种全球知识库网络，能充当研究成果获取、认证、质量评估和进一步重用的基础。随着我们从开放获取向开放科学迈进，通过支持包含科研数据在内的大量研究成果的传播和保存，知识库将成为研究中更为重要的组成部分。此外，知识库已做好准备来支持一种新的学术交流模式，该模式反映出知识随着时间的持续流动，而不是当前的静态情景。

随着越来越多的资助机构采纳依赖知识库基础设施的开放获取和开放科学政策，在知识库和资助团体之间建立更为密切的关系并探求开展定期对话的机制很是关键。此外，鉴于各地区在政策和基础设施方面有着不同做法，那么在共同向前推进时，考虑到观念的多元化是很重要的。COAR及其成员和合作伙伴制定了一条持续且动态的学术交流未来行动路线，欢迎与全球研究理事会做进一步讨论。

2 COAR 的实践与努力

2.1 COAR 发布知识库互操作路线图

2015 年 2 月 5 日，COAR 发布有关知识库互操作的路线图：《知识库互操作的未来指南》。该指南确定了面向知识库团体的重要发展趋势及其相关行动要点，将会协助 COAR 确定未来知识库互操作工作的优先领域。以下为该路线图的执行摘要部分。

在过去的几年间，开放获取知识库及其相关服务已经成为全球数字化研究基础设施的一个重要组成部分。知识库正在不断地与其他系统相结合，如科研管理系统及科研数据知识库，旨在为各种团体提供一整套的更加集成和无缝化的服务。知识库同时还与网络相连接（如国家和地区层面的），以支持统一获取一个开放的、聚合的、可以被机器挖掘到的学术和相关资料的集合，这个集合可以使研究者以新的方式处理工作内容，并能允许资助者和机构追踪科研产出情况。

学术信息交流正在经历着根本性的变革，特别是对科研产出开放获取带来的新需求、同行评议的新形式及测量影响力的新方法。与此同时，还有技术的发展，特别是在通信和接口技术上，这些技术可以促进在相关应用程序和系统间的双向数据交换。本路线图的目的就是确定重要趋势及其相关行动要点，从而帮助知识库团体决定其未来在互操作工作上投入的优先领域。

本路线图以一份全面的关于互操作问题的列表汇编为开端，这些问题是由信息、出版和知识库团体经过广泛讨论得出的。然后，一个专家咨询小组根据这些问题的复杂性和时间相关性的等级，对问题进行排序。本报告显示了这一处理过程的结果，即根据这些维度对问题进行的排序。表 2–1 以二维结构的形式呈现出这些关键方面。

表 2–1　知识库相关互操作问题汇编

	短期	中期	长期
低复杂性	•公开引文格式 •支持数据导出功能 •支持作者标识系统 •支持搜索引擎最优化（SEO） •公开出版物列表 •集成不同的永久标识符	•公开永久标识符 •支持授权和认证 •提升平台稳定性 •支持机构服务 •扩展用户端可用性 •确认知识库元数据 •支持知识库注册可视化 •支持 OAI 服务提供者使用 •集成可用性服务 •支持嵌入式服务 •支持知识库排名系统	

续表

	短期	中期	长期
中复杂性	•公开文献计量信息	•公开版本控制信息 •消除副本（重复存储版本） •改进注册表基础结构 •监管强制遵守开放获取	
高复杂性	•公开使用资料 •支持附加元数据格式	•出版科研数据 •提升元数据质量（数据管护） •处理相关全文 •支持存储协议 •确定知识库及其互操作的结构化建议 •支持高水平出版	•扩展可视化工具的使用 •支持关联（开放）数据 •扩展 / 更换元数据公开协议 •处理复杂 / 复合 / 嵌套的知识库对象 •支持长期保存和存档

通过这一处理过程，有 9 个复杂性各异的问题被列为亟待解决的问题。这些问题可以看作代表目前互操作领域最需要优先处理的问题。

COAR 已经在多个优先领域为提升互操作性而努力，包括作者标识系统、出版物列表、永久标识符、使用资料和文献计量格式。在 2014 年秋天，COAR 与主要的区域知识库网络成立了一个国际性的工作小组，包括 CASRAI 和

EUROCRIS，它们致力于构建一个互操作蓝图，旨在建立一个正式的机制，在该机制下这些互操作问题可以被讨论和解决。

但是，提升互操作性仍然存在许多挑战。9个问题之中的很多问题都牵涉某些程度上的标准化，包括词汇、元数据和指标，这些不仅存在于知识库环境下，还存在于其他系统中。因此，这些领域的互操作性将需要跨国和跨地区及不同团体的其他系统的合作。为了实现互操作性，知识库团体必须与这些其他团体合作并参与到同他们正在进行的对话中。此外，确保本地个体知识库层面的指导方针和标准的实施也是十分困难的，这常常需要大量的团体扩展来提高对于采用标准的好处的认识。一个策略就是与知识库平台开发者合作，将标准执行到知识库软件系统中。同时，知识库的有效接口和相应系统应当开放，实现双向的交流和信道，以允许增强系统的互操作性。

尽管存在这些挑战，未来知识库服务的成功将依靠本地（如机构）、国家和国际不同利益相关者间的无缝联盟。凭借其全球化开放获取知识库网络的视角，COAR将继续致力于实现更为强大的互操作性，不仅包括知识库团体，还包括学术交流系统中的其他成员。

2.2 COAR 启动制定控制词表草案

开放获取知识库在他们扮演的角色和他们表达记录的属性方面不断变化。用户想了解用于描述知识库项目的额外元素，如开放获取状态、研究资助者、所属机构等。考虑到研究趋向国家化和协作性，知识库必须相互链接，并与相关政策和最佳实践保持一致，而标准的受控词表对一致性方面是非常重要的。通过国际编委会的活动，COAR 开始制定一系列开放获取知识库的受控词表。

该项工作旨在建立针对开放获取知识库词表的国际共识。国际编委会已经修订了区域性的和领域性的元数据框架，其中包括 info:eu-repo（和 OpenAIRE 指南）、美国国家信息标准协会（NISO）获取与许可指标、RIOXX、CERIF 语义词表、Casrai 词典等。对于其中的每一个词表元素都会提供一个定义，这些元素已被翻译成多种语言并且将通过关联数据原则与外部资源进行链接。

作为工作的第一步，国际编委会正在制定控制词表草案第一版，同时接受来自各团体的反馈和建议。COAR 邀请大家对英文版的及其他语言版本的（加泰罗尼亚语、汉语、法语、意大利语、葡萄牙语、西班牙语、德语和俄语）词表项、定义进行反馈、建议。所有的反馈都将通过 COAR 的网站进行发布、参考。接收反馈的期限是从 2015 年 8 月 1 日到

2015 年 10 月 1 日的 2 个月。

在接下来的几个月的时间里，国际编委会修订其他的词表，同时这些词表也会对团体开放接收反馈。这项工作将会有利于 COAR 的更宏大目标的实现，这个目标就是开发并维护一些面向开放获取知识库的国际控制词表，并保证它们被广泛地采用。

关于“The Resource Type Vocabulary Draft v.1.0 (July 2015)”可以下载，请至 http://www.coar-repositories.org/activities/repository-interoperability/ig-controlled-vocabularies-for-repository-assets/deliverables/。

这项工作得到 COAR Controlled Vocabularies Editorial Board 及 COAR Interest Group Controlled Vocabularies for Repository Assets 的支持，得到 University of Tor Vergata 人工智能研究及联合国粮食及农业组织在专家和基础设施上对 COAR 词表特别是关联开放数据的支持。

2.3 COAR 参与欧洲 OpenAIRE 2020 以强化国际合作

资助者和研究机构已经把科研成果开放获取作为一种重要机制，以此来刺激创新和创造一个公平的竞争环境。欧盟委员会一直走在开放获取的最前沿，并采纳了一项综合的 OA 政策，要求免费开放受资助研究产生的所有文章。OpenAIRE 2020 是一项用于开发和维护基础设施以支撑欧盟 OA 政策的受资助项目。

COAR 很高兴宣布将参与 OpenAIRE 2020 项目，走国际化知识库网络路线，这将成为 COAR 的重中之重。COAR 将肩负“国际化路线”的重任，使我们能够进一步支持 COAR 正在紧张进行的工作，以便于在主要知识库网络（如 La Referencia、OpenAIRE 和 SHARE 等）之间实现更好的互操作。此外，COAR 将继续提高知识库网络的可见性，并以此作为提供科研成果开放获取的一种可持续选择。

这是一个涉及多方面因素的宏大项目。它通过国家开放获取平台（National Open Access Desks，NOADs）网络为地方层面开放获取的实施提供支持，它还解决了学术界的诸多问题，包括同行评议、计量指标、数据共享的法律考量和关联数据。另外是支持欧共体开放研究数据试点，并为支持研究人员共享数据的机构提供相关培训。

该项目于 2015 年 1 月 28 日、29 日在希腊雅典启动。来自 50 多个合作机构的 100 多名参与者相约雅典来讨论工作计划，确保所有参与者了解这一宏大项目的诸多不同方面。出席开幕式的有 La Referencia（关注 9 个国家开放获取运动的拉美计划）的执行秘书 Alberto Cabezas、COAR 的执行董事 Margaret Kathleen Shearer 和 COAR 的办公室主任 Katharina Mueller。

2.4 COAR 执行董事出席 2015 年国际图联大会

COAR 执行董事 Margaret Kathleen Shearer 出席了国际图联于 2015 年 8 月 15—21 日在南非开普敦举办的 2015 年国际图联大会。本次会议有来自世界各地的超过 3000 名代表参会，是一个与业界同僚沟通交流的绝佳机会，同时还可以继续提高 COAR 在国际图书馆界的知名度。

Daisy Selematsela（COAR 执行董事会成员和隶属于南非国家研究基金会的知识管理企业的执行董事）和 Kathleen 在会上报告了他们合作的关于 COAR 调整知识库网络协议和南非开放获取政策及知识库环境的论文。

Kathleen 还和科学数据联盟（Research Data Alliance，RDA）组织和主持了有关图书馆和科学数据的座谈会。座谈会讨论了区域和机构层面的图书馆科学数据管理。很多 COAR 的成员，包括哥廷根大学的 Wolfram Horstmann、南非开普半岛科技大学的 Zanele Mathe 及南非国家研究基金会的 Daisy Selematsela 都参加了会议。会议摘要可以在普渡大学的 Michael Witt 为本次会议准备的分发资料中找到，内容主题为“图书馆可以做的有关科学数据的 23 件事”（https://rd-alliance.org/system/files/documents/23Things_Libraries_For_Data_RDA.pdf）。

随之，来自研究图书馆协会（Association of Research

Library，ARL）和加拿大研究图书馆协会（Canadian Association of Research Libraries，CARL）的 Kathleen 报告了关于 SHARE 项目和 Portage（一个基于科学数据管理网络的图书馆）的论文。

2.5 La Referencia 采纳《OpenAIRE 指南》

COAR 成员 La Referencia（拉丁美洲开放获取机构知识库网络）采纳《OpenAIRE 指南》中的主要元素，旨在提高全球范围内的互操作性。La Referencia 是一个倡导公共科学和技术的组织，其中包含 9 个成员国家，提供区域性开放获取知识库采集服务。

在 2012 年，La Referencia 选择采纳《Driver 2.0 指南》，并在 2012 年中期就其在 10 个字段的实施机制达成一致。在近 3 年后，新的 La Referencia 指南（La Referencia 国家节点的互操作性元数据和采集政策）诞生并对多个字段进行了更为详细的格式更新，同时提供了对 Drive 中出现的所有字段的建议。他们还提供来自于 OpenAIRE（目前负责维护指南）的说明和修改，并确定了未来推广的主要工作区域。

这项努力作为 La Referencia 工作计划的一部分始于 2014 年年中，并通过 OpenAIRE 2020 项目中的 RedCLARA 实现。该计划于 2015 年启动，其目标之一是“创建一个国际性的

OA 知识库网络以支持全球研究和学术交流”。作为由 COAR 主导的 OpenAIRE 2020 工作包的一部分，其目标是“通过提升协作推动当前互操作领域的活动，同时促进良好实践交流及跨区域网络之间共享指标、服务和技术的采纳”。

指南文档的主要受众是 La Referencia 中的 8 个国家节点。这其中的一些联盟（取决于字段）有可能将实现 La Referencia 级别节点和国家级别节点的转换。同时，它还为区域知识库提供了一个能够实现国际性互操作的路线图，同时允许从国家层面决定实施的细节和进展。

中心元素

La Referencia 全体代表一致同意，最大的变化是将“权利”（dc：rights）字段强制化。这意味着 La Referencia 采集到的每一份文档应该包含一项获取状态的明确声明，该声明基于国际性词表及我们在该领域的传统，同时，只有接受 openAccess（开放获取）或 embargoedAccess（延时开放获取）的文章才会被 La Referencia 采集。关于许可协议，La Referencia 推荐使用知识共享协议。

openAccess（开放获取）：无限制地获取。

embargoedAccess（延时获取）：资源在一定时期内访问受限，直到在某一时间点实现开放。

对于其他字段，在适当的条件下我们赞同：

如果适用，描述、主题、语言和出版者字段，将由推荐变为强制。

如果适用，贡献者字段将被包含在推荐的字段中，并且论文的主管或指导者将成为强制性的。

关系、覆盖范围和受众字段是可选择的（正如 Drive2.0 和 OpenAIRE）。

推荐采纳 dc 字段的格式。

2.6 为评估出版商知识库服务提出准则

许多期刊出版商已经开始为知识库团体提供服务。不同出版商提供的服务可能有所不同，但是通常包括将内容［元数据和（或）论文］自动推送到知识库的服务。

COAR 采用了以下指导方针来帮助成员对这些服务做出明智的决定。这些指南基于知识库团体的价值观和目标，通过可持续的开放获取知识库网络让他们可以实现研究成果开放获取。

COAR 建议，知识库与出版商签订的协议应当满足下列条件：

（1）服务应包括将全文和元数据推送到知识库中，并且推送工作要在发布之前或发布时进行。但如果只是从知识库的元数据链接到出版商付费获取论文全文的网站，则只是提高了出版商的网站流量，并不能提高可获取性。

（2）服务实施时滞期的时间不应该超过12个月（在科学、技术和药品等领域较为理想的一般是6个月），而现有出版发行商不应因提供了知识库存储服务就延长时滞期。

鼓励知识库寻求时滞期过后允许对内容重用和文本挖掘的许可协议。

2.7 强化构建全球开放获取知识空间的目标

全球主要的开放获取知识库网络举办会议，旨在发展更加紧密的关系，并进一步协同其不断扩大的知识库网络。该会议由COAR于2015年4月16日在葡萄牙波尔图举办，并涵盖来自非洲、亚洲、欧洲、拉丁美洲及北美洲的代表。在关于实施开放获取和研究基础设施可持续方式的全球热烈的讨论中，与会者强化了他们的目标来促进反映不同地区方法和能力多样性的解决方案。

知识库网络正在世界各地被开发，用于支持研究成果的开放获取。然而，考虑到研究的国际性和协作性，这些网络必须连接起来，并与有关问题如政策、标准和服务保持一致。在这次会议上，与会代表分享了他们本地网络的更新。许多网络在过去一年中有显著的改进，现在处于一个更好的时机来深入合作。该团体还审查了自他们去年的会议以来知识库网络活动的进展情况。自上一年工作以来的具体产出包括：发表反对时滞期的联合声明，启动一个技术工作组努力协调开放获取元素和元数据架构，以及提高世界范围内知识库网络的知名度。

与会者还讨论了在未来一年中进一步调整其网络的优先事项。活动将包括围绕准则和工具发展更密切的合作，以及网络之间被建议的一些双边合作。此外，与会者一致认为，交流战略被制定来继续提高知识库网络作为关键基础设施组件的知名度。也有人表示支持进一步与政策制定者和其他利益相关者合作以确保采用平衡的开放获取政策。

COAR 将与社会各界合作来完成未来一年中的活动。与会者名单和有关会议的报告将很快在 COAR 网站公布。

3 COAR 取得的合作与成果

3.1 主要知识库网络同意开展合作

2015 年 7 月 9—10 日，三大区域开放获取知识库网络和整合者（OpenAire、La Referencia 和 SHARE）同开放获取知识库联盟（COAR）和开放科学中心（COS）在弗吉尼亚州的夏洛茨维尔会见，共同讨论协同效应和潜在的合作领域。

开放获取知识库正在被世界各地所采纳，以支持和促进开放科学发展，通过科研产出的免费获取使科研投入最大化发挥作用已成为一种趋势。这其中的很多知识库通过区域整合者相连接，构成了可持续的分布式知识库网络，这种知识库网络可以提供对科研和学者创造的有价值信息的获取和保存。

然而，科研是国际化的，科研人员需要跨地区和大洲合作以解决最为重要的世界性难题，如气候变化、医疗卫生、经济等。这次会议的目标是确保区域知识库网络更加互补和互相协调，以及共同创建一个无缝的全球性网络。

这次会议成果颇丰，显现出三大知识库网络在目标、技术和用例上已达成高度一致，并且具有强烈的合作意愿。特别是本次会议还确定了三大知识库网络将在以下一些具体领域进行合作：

常规数据交换：交换数据和制定跨管辖区域的采集和整合协议将拓展区域的覆盖范围及提高效率。

通用元数据和词表：努力争取在利用关键元数据元素和通用词表描述资助者和所属机构、开放获取状态和项目标识等方面达成一致。这将有助于已经开展的旨在开发通用元数据元素的 COAR-CASRAI 工作，并将支持知识库管理者更好地标引其资源。

通用技术服务：评估采纳通用代理 / 路由器技术及其他服务的可行性。

持续性对话：定期会晤以共享有关技术和战略挑战的方法和观点。

在接下来的几周内，COAR 将与三大知识库网络制定一份更加详细的计划以实现这些特定目标。

3.2 可持续发展网络论坛的讨论

2015 年 9 月，联合国粮食与农业组织、国际图书馆协会联合会和开放获取知识库联盟联合举办了可持续发展目标网络论坛讨论会。

在论坛举办的12天里，参会人员讨论了关于包括开放获取在内的信息获取在可持续发展中的作用。参会人员提供了大量范例、说明和案例研究来证明信息获取和开放获取提高了人们的生活水平。信息获取和开放获取是一个交叉问题，它支撑了大部分甚至全部的可持续发展目标，应该被看作是实现可持续发展目标的关键因素之一。促进信息获取的政策是多样化的，而且在很大程度上是由当地的环境决定的。显然，获得各国政府支持需要时间，但是会很有效果。尽管我们的观点存在差异，但整个社会能够从经验和成功案例的分享中受益。讨论的档案可以在这里获取：https://dgroups.org/fao/ciard-econsultation/sdgs-impact-access-information-societies/。

论坛举办期间，我们有4份展示作品，分别来自：Stuart Hamilton、Jean Claude Guédon、Leslie Chan 和 Ellen Namhila。研讨会的资料在FAO网站上都可以获取：http://aims.fao.org/capacity-development/webinars。我们还收到了联合国秘书长特别顾问Amina Mohammed女士预先录制的关于2015年以后发展规划的短视频，题名叫作《可持续发展目标与信息的获取》，见 https://www.youtube.com/watch?v=-6KMQV9VYg4&feature=youtu.be。

这次电子论坛上，一个重要的认识愈加清晰，那就是开放获取知识库在支持世界各地可持续发展中起到了非常重要的作用。开放获取不仅提供了获取发表在不易获取的基于预定的期刊上的知识和信息的方法，同时也为各地基础设施的建设及全世界各机构的能力建设做出了贡献。开放获取确保知识是在原始状态下保存。我们不应该低估为创造一个更加持续、开放的知识共享空间而建设的分布式网络的价值。

然而，还有很多事情要做。因为国际期刊系统自身的声望，所以大部分研究人员都非常希望在上面发表论文，这种现象扭曲了议题的国家研究规划对西欧和北美的重要性。一些出席者谈到用知识库解决这一问题并且创造一个更加公平的体系。但是这意味着扩大知识库的作用，使其不仅提供获取知识的途径，而且提供增值服务，如同行评议。

在即将到来的几个月里，我们希望获得更多更广泛的关于开放获取知识库的建议，还有用来评估是否可取且对我们的社会有利的增值服务。我们欢迎来自社会各界的更多想法。

3.3 国际主要知识库组织同意采用通用指南

全世界逐渐认识到，如果研究成果能够被广泛共享和公开提供给每一个人，那么我们大量的研发投资将产生更大效益。La Referencia、OpenAIRE 和 COAR 重申了对共享愿景的大力支持，他们的共同愿景是将全球知识库组织作为基础设施，提供具有可持续性的开放获取研究成果，以确保所有研究人员和公民能够访问公共资助的研究成果。

2015 年 11 月 25—26 日，来自 La Referencia、OpenAIRE 和 COAR 的代表们齐聚里约热内卢，讨论实施通用元数据指南的问题，以便在知识库组织和识别领域取得进一步合作。

OenAIRE 和 La Referencia 代表着世界上最先进的 2 个开放获取知识库区域组织。这两大网络之间的密切合作将提高组织中共同内容的可用性和可见性，促进这 2 个区域增值服务的发展。

因此，这 3 家组织决心通过以下活动实现共同的愿景：

- La Referencia 和 OpenAIRE 将基于当前的 OpenARIE 指南和在 COAR 背景下创建的词汇，实施知识库组织通用元数据指南，并将合作开发这些指南。

- COAR、La Referencia 和 OpenAIRE 将探索建立管理拉丁美洲知识库和知识库组织能力的方法，尤其是在探索最佳实践方面。

- 在 COAR 协助下，La Referencia 和 OpenAIRE 将继续与其他国家和区域组织共同推进全球知识库组织愿景的实现，调查支持开放获取和开放科学的公共服务。

- La Referencia 是 8 个拉丁美洲国家的开放获取知识库网络。它通过 La Referencia_OpenAIRE_Workshop2015_Mosaicostandards 及一站式探索发现平台，支持拉丁美洲的国家开放获取战略。La Referencia 从国家节点来收割学术论文和学位论文，来自大学和研究机构的知识库。该倡议建立在公共科学与技术（国家科技部）和 RedCLARA 的技术和组织协议上。

● OpenAIRE 受到欧盟 Horizon 2020 项目资助，作为欧洲科研的开放获取基础设施，建立在开放获取知识库网络的基础上。

具体协议：

● La Referencia 的各成员国将采用 OpenAIRE 指南，并且随着未来的不断发展，他们将通过 La Referencia 参与到指南的制定中。

● La Referencia 将制定战略并创建实践社区，以促进参与国范围内的经验共享，支持在地方机构中的指南实施。

● La Referencia、OpenAIRE 和 COAR 将合作开发一种混合式学习课程，以建立管理拉丁美洲知识库的能力。

● La Referencia 和 OpenAIRE 将提供验证器，用于评估知识库对指南的遵守程度。

参与者：

● Amaro, Bianca – Ibict，巴西

● Amórtegui, Miguel Ángel – RENATA，哥伦比亚

● Apollaro, Alberto – Mincyt，阿根廷

● Azrilevich, Paola – La Referencia/Mincyt，阿根廷

● Cabezas, Alberto – La Referencia，智利

- Granados, Diana – Colciencias，哥伦比亚
- Labbé, Carmen Gloria – COAR/RedCLARA，智利
- Matas, Lautaro – La Referencia，阿根廷
- Merino, Sonia Elsy – Min. de Educación，萨尔瓦多
- Muñoz, Patricia – CONACYT，智利
- Rasseli, Luiz Alberto – La Referencia，巴西
- Recavarren, Isabel – Concytec，秘鲁
- Ribeiro, Washington – Ibict，巴西
- Rodrigues, Eloy – OpenAIRE/COAR/ Minho University，葡萄牙
- Shearer, Kathleen – COAR，加拿大
- Siguencia, Josefina – CEDIA，厄瓜多尔

4 发展战略及计划

4.1 COAR 2016—2018 年发展战略

愿景

基于开放获取数字知识库组织的可持续、全球性知识共享。

目标

通过以国际合作与协同为基础的开放获取知识库全球网络来提升科研成果的可见性与利用程度。

COAR 2016—2018 年战略发展方向

为了实现我们的使命及以上愿景，COAR 将专注于团体、领导力及在国际层面上的联合。

引领 COAR 活动的 4 个战略发展方向：

（1）促进作为国际科研基础设施关键要素的可持续、全球性开放获取知识库组织的发展，从而为科研与教育活动提供卓越的支持。

（2）支持开放获取知识库团体，并培养本地发展和管理知识库及知识库组织的能力。

（3）为知识库、知识库组织与其他相关系统制定和促进提升互操作性、共同标准与最佳实践。

（4）促进知识库及知识库组织增值业务的发展和应用。

4.2 COAR 2016—2017 年工作计划

2016—2017 年，COAR 将通过以下工作计划来实现其战略目标。

该工作计划将在 2017 年年初进行审议，以确保在快速变化的环境中保持目标与行动的一致。

1. 促进作为国际科研基础设施关键要素的可持续、全球性开放获取知识库组织的发展

目标	行动	相关人员
提升知识库组织对重要利益相关者团体的价值	•参加相关会议，阐述 COAR 的工作与愿景 •（在适当时机）参加联系人之间和其他在线论坛的讨论 •参加工作小组及反映 COAR 战略目标的其他相关行动 •支持区域知识库组织建设，为科学出版物、数据及其他资源提供高效、可持续的开放获取接入基础设施 •与开放获取团体及组织合作，促进 COAR 愿景与目标的实现 •与其他国际组织合作，如全球科研委员会及联合国教科文组织 •为开放获取知识库的相关政策、法律的制定和实施提供支持	•执行理事 •执行委员会 •COAR 学科专家 •知识库标准化委员会 •COAR 办公室

拓展 COAR 会员	•在关于知识库社区重要性的问题上公开联合 •广泛宣传 COAR 开展的工作 •参加其他组织的活动将提升 COAR 外部形象 •通过针对性的营销和传播活动（内部的和外部的）巩固完善 COAR 品牌 •着手建立机构招募新的成员 •制订能清晰描述旨在增加会员、筹款、提升知名度等活动的详细计划	•执行理事 •COAR 办公室 •执行委员会 •COAR 成员
成为重要国际电子基础设施和学术交流活动的关键性利益相关者	•参与机构内部管理及关于组织基础设施、开放获取及学术交流行动的外部磋商	•执行理事 •执行委员会

2. 支持开放获取知识库团体，并培养地方发展和管理知识库及知识组织的能力

目标	行动	相关人员
为构建开放获取知识库及知识库组织的开发和管理能力提供支持	•结合会员大会策划活动、研讨会 •为 COAR 成员策划特定的主题日 •参加研究数据联盟并与成员们分享相关信息 •为知识库管理者制定培训课程，特别关注发展中国家 •使用第三方资金启动工作人员交流项目 •与 COAR 成员机构合作伙伴启动一个试点项目以支持知识传递、信息共享及工作人员交流	•执行理事 •执行委员会 •COAR 学科专家

发展国际知识库管理的最佳实践方式	•调查发展开放获取知识库管理的全球性质量标准的潜力	•执行理事 •执行委员会 •可能开展该项活动的 COAR 小组

3. 制定和推动知识库、知识库组织与其他相关系统的互用性、共同标准及最佳实践方式

目标	行动	相关人员
提高地区和国家知识库组织的标准化水平	•开发和维护一套知识库的国际性受控词表 •通过 COAR-CASRAI 工作小组讨论并协调一致采用共同的词汇表和元数据框架 •促进知识库组织之间的交流，支持这些组织间的双边活动	•COAR 受控词表利益相关团体 / 编委会 •执行理事 •知识库组织标准化战略委员会 •COAR-CASRAI 元数据工作小组 •各组织协调代表
在知识库和其他系统之间实现更大的互用性	•提升 COAR 的互用性发展路线图的知名度 •与其他利益相关者及团体合作协调一致的元数据标准	•执行理事 •COAR 学科专家 •COAR 受控词表利益相关团体 / 编委会
提高知识库内容通过搜索引擎检索的可发现性	•为谷歌搜索引擎及谷歌学术制定知识库指南	•承担这一活动的 COAR 小组
开展关于研究数据管理知识库及系统间互操作性	•参加研究数据联盟，致力于开发出版物与数据知识库之间可互用的元数据及词表	•执行理事 •COAR 学科专家

4. 促进知识库及知识库组织增值业务的发展和应用

目标	行动	相关人员
跟踪增值业务的发展趋势	•跟踪并与 COAR 团体成员分享知识库新功能使用情况统计	•COAR 的使用数据和非利益相关方团体
为建设中的知识库制订可持续发展策略	•在出版商许可范围内收集、共享、促进开放获取条款的实施	•执行理事 •许可协议工作组
识别需求并推进新的知识库服务项目	•启动一个在知识库组织顶层采取同行评议服务的试点项目 •与 COAR 成员分享关于知识库不断发展新服务的信息 •制定关于研究数据管理的 COAR 发展蓝图（可能与 RDA 图书馆的研究数据利益相关团体合作）	•执行理事 •执行委员会 •COAR 学科专家
积极促进下一代知识库的发展和应用	•与知识库平台开发者及知识库团体合作来促进反映科技环境不断变化的新架构、协议、功能特性的应用	•执行理事 •执行委员会 •可能承担该活动的 COAR 小组

5 关于 COAR

5.1 关于 COAR

COAR，即开放获取知识库联盟，是一个年轻的、迅速成长的知识库联盟。COAR 成立于 2009 年 10 月，联合了全球 100 多家机构（包括欧洲、拉丁美洲、亚洲和南美洲）。它的使命是通过开放获取知识库的全球网络，扩大研究成果的可见度，促进研究成果的广泛应用。

通过各成员机构的共同努力，COAR 致力于发展成为一个全球开放获取知识库共同体，汇集跨国家、地区和学科领域的实践经验。COAR 的愿景是构建一个连接全球开放获取知识库的知识基础设施。目前，COAR 有 3 个工作组，每个组都有自己的责任、目标和相关活动。

5.2 加入 COAR 的权益

成员机构除了拥有在各自领域的高级访问权限以外，还能显著节约经费和时间成本，减少机构、国家和区域等层面工作人员在诸如系统和技术市场分析、实施建设方案等工作上的投入。

成员机构可以参加国际或区域知识共享活动，如 COAR 专门为会员举办的论坛 / 研讨会。成员机构可以通过参加聚焦小组，与来自世界各地的同行进行专门的、深入的和富有成果的经验交流。

通过参加 COAR 工作组的工作，成员机构有机会和国际最佳实践者一起，参与和投入到国际开放获取知识库活动当中。借助于 COAR 许可工作组或 COAR 知识库观察等相关的国际行动，成员机构将站在 OA 知识库发展的最前沿。

COAR 提供个性化的帮助 / 指导服务，帮助成员机构负责主办或承办 COAR 会议，并为发展中地区提供赞助。成员机构可以通过参与 COAR 相关研究、路线图等工作，推进 OA 知识库的发展。

5.3 加入 COAR

5.3.1 会员种类

（1）正式会员：具有法律实体意义的高等教育、研究、基础设施和技术等机构。包括：

①单独会员：有选举权、被选举权、发言权和建议权。

②团体会员：图书馆组织、专业协会和联盟及由上述组织组成的机构。还包括国家图书馆协会和机构知识库组织。

有被选举权、发言权和建议权。

（2）特别会员：若干不发达的国家（名单见 http://www.un.org/ohrlls/）。如果名单之外的其他地区的机构想要申请特别会员资格，可向执行委员会提出申请并说明自身的困难。有被选举权、发言权和建议权。经过申请，可以获得选举权。

（3）荣誉会员：为 COAR 提供特殊服务促进协会发展的人。具有的权利同特别会员一样。

（4）合作伙伴：从事与 COAR 的任务和目标有关活动的机构。具有参与会议及发言的权利。

5.3.2 如何成为 COAR 会员

（1）提交申请表

地址见 https://www.coar-repositories.org/files/COAR_application_form_2014.pdf，并以信件的形式寄给 COAR 办公室，地址：

COAR e.V.

at Goettingen State and University Library

Platz der Goettinger Sieben 1

D-37073 Goettingen, Germany。

（2）每年定期交付会员费

①单独会员：500 欧元。

②团体会员（表 5–1）：

表 5–1 团体会员费用

机构数量 / 个	每个成员机构享受的折扣	每个成员机构的费用 / 欧元	每个联盟最低费用 / 欧元	每个联盟最高费用 / 欧元
11~30	10%	450	4950	13 500
31~50	20%	400	12 400	20 000
51~70	30%	350	17 850	24 500
71 及以上	35%	325	23 075	

注：执行委员会有权对来自同一国家的大范围联盟给予特殊的折扣，需要申请者在执行委员会会议开始前至少 1 周提交申请。

③特别会员：可以免去定期的会员费，但是需要为活动做出贡献。

④荣誉会员：不做财务贡献。

⑤合作伙伴：提供赞助。

5.3.3 加入会员流程

在章程会议上，会员自主选择成为正式会员还是特殊会员。

申请以书面的形式交给执行委员会，如果申请被拒绝，申请书将被转交下一届大会。

由执行委员会推荐，并且经过 2/3 人数通过，申请者将成为荣誉会员。

5.4 常见问题及解答

5.4.1 关于 COAR

（1）什么是开放获取知识库联盟（COAR）？

COAR 是一个联合了来自于世界各组织的年轻联盟。它的核心任务是通过一个开放获取数字知识库的全球网络，扩大研究成果的可见度，促进研究成果的广泛应用。此外，COAR 的目标是让世界的每位公民能够从公共资助的研究产出中获取知识，或者从中获益。

（2）COAR 是如何开始的？

成立 COAR 的想法要追溯到 2005—2009 年欧盟委员会资助的欧盟 DRIVE 项目（Digital Repository Infrastructure Vision for Europe，欧洲数字知识库基础设施展望，http://www.driver-repository.eu）。在该项目的咨询过程中发现，包含机构和组织的国际知识库共同体的组织模式是非常有必要的，因此，为了促进全球知识库共同体和世界各地的虚拟知识库网络的实现，于 2009 年 9 月成立了 COAR。

（3）COAR 的主要目标是什么？

- 通过 OA 知识库扩大研究成果的可见度。
- 作为知识库及其网络、国家和国际层面的基于电子基础设施知识库的展示途径。
- 确定和推广知识库的内容缴存策略，并促进与出版商的共识。

- 与致力于知识库标准化和互操作性的知识库共同体开展紧密合作。
- 为知识库管理者和从业人员提供专业咨询及交流机会。

（4）COAR 会员的主要权益是什么？

COAR 为会员和合作伙伴提供很多权益，主要是：

- 共享全球知识库共同体及其网络发展的经验和最佳实践。
- 共享知识库存缴策略与创建内容临界规模。
- 发展与不同相关利益方的合作（如出版商）。
- 为交流与发展相关资料、举办培训等活动做出贡献并从中获益。

（5）COAR 代表哪里？

COAR 代表来自包括欧洲、拉丁美洲、亚洲和北美洲的 24 个国家的 90 个机构。

（6）COAR 是如何管理的？

COAR 由执行董事支持下的执行董事会及 COAR 办公室管理。更多信息可在 COAR 章程中找到：https://www.coar-repositories.org/about-coar/articles-of-association/。

（7）COAR 的资金来源是什么？

COAR的资金来源于会员费、赞助商和会员的各种资助。

5.4.2 COAR 的活动

（1）我能为 COAR 的活动做些什么？

COAR 有兴趣与机构和组织分享其使命和目标。访问 COAR 的网站，了解更多 COAR 工作组当前的活动，并与 COAR 联系，讨论进一步合作的机会。

（2）我怎么才能加入工作组？

仅限于会员和合作伙伴能成为 COAR 工作组的成员。只要您有兴趣和时间，非常欢迎随时加入 COAR。请通过电子邮件 office@coar-repositories.org 联系 COAR 办公室，自愿加入任何一个工作组。

（3）COAR 如何帮助区域、国家或本地会员来宣传？

COAR 有利于会员和合作伙伴的经验分享。同时根据他们的需求和资源的可用性，提供了进一步的支持措施。

（4）COAR 提高各个知识库之间互操作性的目的是什么？

COAR 目前互操作项目的目标旨在发展全球开放知识库互操作的路线图。该路线图将为支持服务提供指导，包括使用数据统计，补助金申报，通过知识库的互操作标准、协议和指导的引文分析。

5.4.3 加入 COAR

（1）我的机构如何加入 COAR？

会员资格对任何法律实体都是开放的，包括不以营利为目的的高等教育、科研、基础设施和技术的机构。全部会员必须定期支付会员费。

（2）协会都提供哪些会员类型？

本协会有正式会员，可以选择单独的会员资格和团体会员资格。此外，还有特别会员、荣誉会员和合作伙伴。所有的会员和合作伙伴赞同该协会的宗旨。

更多相关信息请参考：https://www.coar-repositories.org/about-coar/articles-of-association/。

（3）什么是年度会员费？

请查阅 COAR 的会员费条例：https://www.coar-repositories.org/member-and-partnership/membership-fee-regulations/。

（4）会员费看起来非常高，没有那么多经费的机构如何加入 COAR？

COAR 鼓励会员以群组形式加入，这样能显著降低会员费。例如，一个有 5 个会员的群组会员费是每年 750 欧元。群组的成员可以从 COAR 的所有活动中获益，但是在每年的会员大会投票中，其组内成员必须取得一致。

（5）谁能成为 COAR 的合作伙伴？

对于那些从事与 COAR 的任务和目标相关联活动的机构，合作关系是开放的。

COAR 的会员主要是非营利机构，同时 COAR 也会邀请私营公司成为其合作伙伴。

（6）在哪里能够找到更多关于会员关系 / 会员费 / 服务等信息?

浏览 COAR 的主页：www.coar-repositories.org/。

通过 Twitter 关注 COAR：twitter.com/COAR_eV。

联系 COAR 办公室：电话：+49 551 39-22215；传真：+49 551 39-5222；电子邮件：office@coar-repositories.org。